Advance praise for *May It Amuse the Court:*

"The book offers entertaining and perceptive insights for the lawyer and layperson alike. *May It Amuse the Court* will make you laugh, if only to keep from crying."
—Nadine Strossen, president of the American Civil Liberties Union

"These are fun, but they are more than that—they interpret and get to the point for the layman as the legalistic language of opinions often do not. *May It Amuse the Court* allows us to follow the Court's pictorial path from its tangle with racial issues arising from Emancipation to the present. This book, like its many cartoons, will amuse and instruct."
—William S. McFeely, Pulitzer Prize winner, *Grant: A Biography*

"An inspired, fresh look at the highest court in the land and who we are as a people as seen through political cartoons. From the thorny issues of segregation and judicial appointments to prohibition and abortion, *May It Amuse the Court* provides useful commentary alongside political cartoons of the day to give historical context. A fun book for those . . . who know how to laugh and appreciate good political cartoons."
—Diana Daniels, *Washington Post*

"An engaging, irreverent chronicle of the history of political crises confronting the Supreme Court and the country, from the Civil War and Dred Scott to the 2000 presidential election."
—David M. O'Brien, University of Virginia, American Bar Association's Silver Gavel Award-winning author of *Storm Center: The Supreme Court in American Politics*

"If you want to learn U.S. history in an unusual way, read *May It Amuse the Court*. It brings the Constitution and the Supreme Court alive with a collection that sometimes shocks, but mostly which will make you laugh."
—Constance Curry, winner of the Lillian Smith Award, *Silver Rights*

"Effectively using provocative and humorous cartoons to focus on significant and controversial events in the nation's constitutional history, the authors enlighten, educate, and entertain."
—John Curley, CEO, Gannett

"Although some are outrageous and even deeply offensive by contemporary standards, these drawings capture our history—for good and bad--and give us a window into the mind of the times."
—Harvey Rishikof, dean of the Ralph R. Papitto School of Law, Roger Williams University

May It Amuse the Court

Editorial Cartoons of the Supreme Court and Constitution

by Michael A. Kahn and Harry Pohlman

HILL STREET PRESS ⅆ ATHENS, GEORGIA

A HILL STREET PRESS BOOK

Published in the United States of America by Hill Street Press LLC
191 East Broad Street, Suite 209 Athens, Georgia 30601-2848 USA
706.613.7200
info@hillstreetpress.com www.hillstreetpress.com

Front cover image "King of Blunders" appeared in *Judge.*
Cover photograph of the Supreme Court building courtesy of Library of Congress.
Back cover image appeared in *Arizona Republic.*

Text design by Anne Richmond Boston.
Cover design by Anne Richmond Boston and Brandi Goodson.
Printed in the United States of America.

Library of Congress Cataloging-in-Publication Data

Kahn, Michael A., 1949–
May it amuse the court : editorial cartoons of the Supreme Court
and the Constitution /
by Michael A. Kahn and H.L. Pohlman.
p.   cm.
ISBN 1-58818-046-8
1. Constitutional history—United States—Caricatures and cartoons.
2. United States. Supreme Court—Caricatures and cartoons.
3. American wit and humor, Pictorial. I. Pohlman, H. L., 1952– II. Title.

KF4541.Z9K34 2003
347.73'26'0222—dc21   2001024490

10 9 8 7 6 5 4 3 2 1

First printing

CONTENTS

FOREWORD

One measure of a free society is how much leeway it gives its people and its press to criticize its leaders. The enactment of the First Amendment to the United States Constitution was motivated in part by colonial opposition to English prosecutions of "seditious libel"—the "intentional publication, without lawful excuse or justification, of written blame of any public man, or of the law, or of any institution established by law." When the Federalists nonetheless enacted the Sedition Act of 1798 and used it to prosecute Jeffersonian Republicans for "false, scandalous, and malicious writing" about the federal government, they helped seal their own defeat in the 1800 election. Once he was president, Jefferson pardoned all of those convicted under the act, and it expired of its own force in 1801. The notion that seditious libel could ever be prosecuted in the United States faded into history.

Seditious libel was interred once and for all by the Supreme Court's landmark 1964 ruling in *New York Times v. Sullivan*, which set high hurdles for public officials seeking to sue the press for defamation. Writing for the Court, Justice William Brennan reaffirmed "a profound national commitment to the principle that debate on public issues should be uninhibited, robust, and wide-open, and that it may well include vehement, caustic, and sometimes unpleasantly sharp attacks on government and public officials."

In delivering such attacks, few are more deft than political cartoonists, those who cloak their criticisms in humorous satire. And few are more democratic, for the irreverence of political caricature has the effect of deflating any pretensions to majesty or infallibility on the part of public leaders.

The Supreme Court explicitly recognized these qualities of political cartoons in a unanimous 1988 decision, *Hustler Magazine and Larry Flynt v. Jerry Falwell*, which upheld the First Amendment right of a magazine to publish a vulgar ad parody insinuating that a well-known conservative religious minister had had a drunken incestuous rendezvous with his mother in an outhouse—no matter how much emotional distress it might have caused Reverend Falwell. Political cartoonists were alarmed by the case that led up to this decision, fearing that if *Hustler* could be sued for inflicting emotional distress through satire, so could they. The Association of American Editorial Cartoonists went so far as to file an amicus brief in the case.

This effort was clearly influential: In delivering the decision in *Hustler*'s favor, Chief Justice William Rehnquist wrote that "were we to hold otherwise, there can be little doubt that political cartoonists and satirists would be subjected to damages awards. . . . The appeal of the political cartoon or caricature is often based on exploration of unfortunate physical traits or politically embarrassing events—an exploration often calculated to injure the feelings of the subject of the portrayal. The art of the cartoonist is often not reasoned or evenhanded, but slashing and one-sided." The chief justice reviewed the "sometimes caustic nature" of American political cartoons from "the early cartoon portraying George Washington as an ass" through those satirizing "Lincoln's tall, gangling posture, Teddy Roosevelt's glasses and teeth, and Franklin D. Roosevelt's jutting jaw and cigarette holder," concluding that "our political discourse would have been considerably poorer without them."

It would hardly do for the Court that has reaffirmed such freedom to satirize presidents and other public officials to view itself—or the Constitution that protects such freedom—as immune from the political cartoonist's barbs. And the remarkable collection of cartoons that Michael A. Kahn and Harry Pohlman have assembled in this volume demonstrates that in fact neither the high court nor our founding document and its amendments have been spared. The cartoons in this book chronicle through caricature some of the most pointed controversies in American constitutional history, and the text that narrates them brings those controversies to life with great clarity, economy, and verve. Few books could so vividly demonstrate that in our political system, just as no man is above the law, no institution is above the pen—not even the one institution, the Supreme Court, that protects all the others.

KATHLEEN SULLIVAN

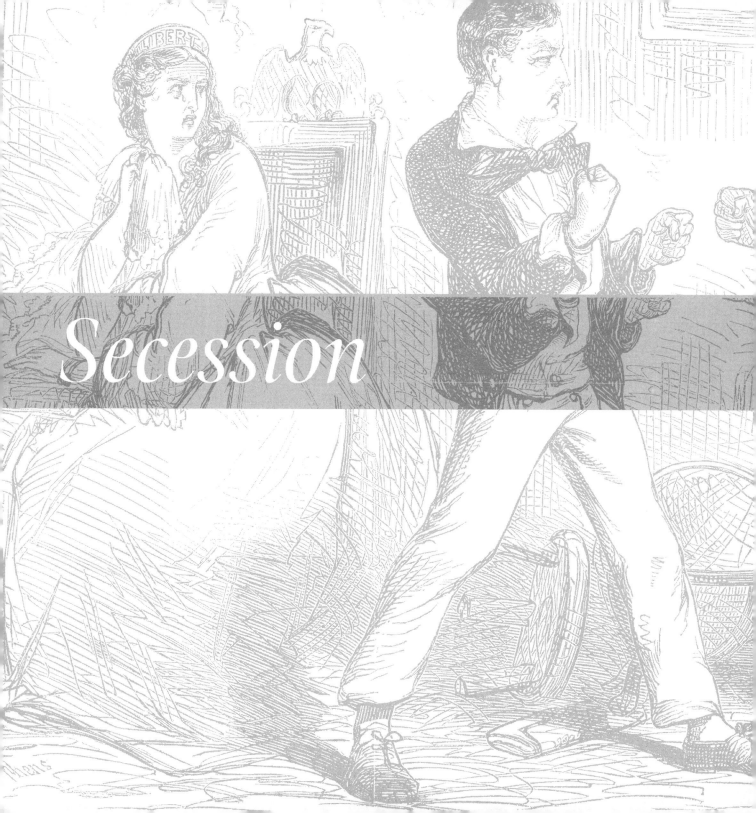

Secession

CHAPTER 1

Secession

Prior to the Civil War, it was unclear how united the United States were. Were the American people bound together into an indissoluble whole or was the Union merely a compact from which states could withdraw at any time? The "peculiar institution" of slavery was the main reason why this question repeatedly arose during the nineteenth century. Could Southern states secede from the Union if Congress barred slavery from the Western federal territories and therefore from future Western states? In the Missouri Compromise of 1820, the North and South agreed that slavery would be prohibited in all parts of the Louisiana Purchase north of the degree of latitude marking Missouri's southern boundary. In the Compromise of 1850, California was admitted as a free state, but New Mexico and Utah Territories were granted the right to come into the Union as either slave or free states and a tough new federal Fugitive Slave Act was enacted. Then, in 1854, Congress enacted a law that repealed the Missouri Compromise and granted Kansas and Nebraska territories the right to decide for themselves whether they would become slave or free states. Settlers from both the North and the South flocked to Kansas to decide the territory's future. Violence soon erupted. By the end of 1856, some two hundred persons had died in "Bleeding Kansas."

The Supreme Court attempted to resolve the constitutional crisis in *Dred Scott v. Sandford* (1857). Dred Scott was the slave of a Missouri army surgeon who had been assigned to duty in Illinois

MISTRESS COLUMBIA, WHO HAS BEEN TAKING A NAP, SUDDENLY WAKES UP AND CALLS HER NOISY SCHOLARS TO ORDER.

and Wisconsin Territory—the former a free state under the Northwest Ordinance, the latter a free territory under the Missouri Compromise of 1820. After his owner died, Scott filed suit for his freedom, claiming that his former residence in Illinois and Wisconsin made him a free man. The Court rejected Scott's argument in a 7 to 2 decision. The justices in the majority issued opinions supporting in varying degrees three conclusions. First, because Scott was an African American, he was not a citizen of the United States and therefore could not sue in federal court. Second, Congress had no power to prohibit slavery in the territories. Third, ownership of slaves was a property right protected by the Due Process Clause of the Fifth Amendment, implying that territorial legislatures also could not prohibit slavery within their borders. The decision, often described as the Supreme Court's greatest "self-inflicted wound," widened the growing gulf separating the North from the South.

The *Dred Scott* decision became an important issue in the famous debates between Republican Abraham Lincoln and Democrat Stephen Douglas during the Illinois senate campaign of 1858 and later in the presidential campaign of 1860. In the debates, Lincoln opposed the decision, arguing that the federal government had clear authority to prevent the spread of slavery into the western territories. Douglas, a proponent of the policy that each territory should decide for itself whether it would become a free or a slave state, attacked Lincoln for not respecting the Supreme Court's role as the ultimate interpreter of the Constitution. Douglas's support of popular sovereignty, however, did not satisfy Southern Democrats. At the Democratic party convention held in Charleston, South Carolina, in April 1860, Southern delegates walked out after their Northern counterparts refused to support resolutions declaring that it was the federal government's duty to protect the property rights of slave holders in the territories. While the Charleston convention nominated Douglas for president, the Southern delegates reconvened in Baltimore and nominated Vice-President John C. Breckenridge as their candidate.

Despite the growing antagonism between the North and South, cartoons of the period retained a tone of optimism that a compromise like those of 1820 and 1850 would be reached and that the Union would therefore be preserved. One such cartoon, published in *Harper's Weekly* on January 7, 1860, compared the political situation to a schoolhouse squabble. The teacher, Miss Columbia, who appears to be a severe disciplinarian, has just awakened from a nap. With a switch in her hand and the Constitution by her side, there seems little doubt that she will be able to quickly "call her noisy scholars to order." Another cartoon, published by Henry Louis Stephens in *Vanity Fair* on March 3, 1860, was also confidant about the future. Alluding to John Milton's *Samson Agonistes,* the cartoon denies that slavery could ever destroy the Union. Though Samson, both in Milton's poem and the original biblical version of the story, was able to pull down the temple's pillars, "Sambo Agonistes" reports that

SAMBO AGONISTES.

DEY DONT " BUDGE"

THE POLITICAL QUADRILLE
Music by Dred Scott

the pillars holding up the American constitutional edifice "don't budge." Both cartoons express the conviction that the Constitution and the Union were strong enough to bear the political strains brought on by the slavery controversy.

An interesting lithograph from an unknown artist reflects the impact the *Dred Scott* decision had on the presidential election of 1860. "The Political Quadrille," depicts the four candidates, each with a partner symbolizing one of his primary constituencies, dancing to the music of *Dred Scott*: Republican Abraham Lincoln, with an African-American woman; Democrat Stephen A. Douglas, with an Irish Catholic; Democrat John C. Breckenridge, with outgoing President James Buchanan (whose nickname was "Buck"); and Constitutional Union party candidate John Bell, with a Native American. The last pairing is puzzling, but perhaps it is a sarcastic reference to the anti-immigrant tendencies

of the Know Nothing Party, the remnants of which tended to support Bell. The general meaning of the cartoon, however, is fairly clear. All the candidates of the 1860 presidential election had to take a stand on the *Dred Scott* decision. It is somewhat unusual for a Supreme Court decision to play such a pivotal role in a presidential election.

The optimism of early 1860 waned significantly by the end of the year. Not only had Southern leaders during the campaign threatened secession if Lincoln was elected president, but the election results revealed how sharply divided the country was: Lincoln did not win a single electoral vote from a Southern state, but won the election by sweeping the Northern and Western states, collecting 180 electoral votes; Breckenridge took seventy-two Southern electoral votes; Bell carried three border states for a total of thirty-nine electors; and Douglas

BROTHER JONATHAN LAME.

Doctor Disunion.—POOR FELLOW! HIS CONSTITUTION IS SO RUN DOWN THAT I FEAR HE CANNOT SURVIVE WITHOUT AN AMPUTATION.
Nurse Columbia.—O! DON'T GIVE IT UP, DOCTOR. GOOD NURSING WILL DO ANYTHING—EVERYTHING—IF YOU WILL ONLY GIVE HIM THE OPPORTUNITY.

the result it most wanted to avoid: the liberation of the black slaves. Just as genies have been known to escape from their bottles, so would secession, in Stephens's opinion, bring about the abolition of slavery in the Southern states. Though it took years of fighting and an amendment to the Constitution, Stephens's prediction was eventually borne out. The snakes wrapped around the "rising Afrite," however, give the impression that Stephens did not favor emancipation, which would not be all that surprising since the number of abolitionists at the beginning of the war was relatively small. Lincoln himself, in a speech prior to the Civil War, expressed his opinion that the federal government had no authority to restrict slavery in the South, though he hoped, if only because "a house divided

ended up with twelve electoral votes. A cartoon drawn by Andrew Filmer and published in *Vanity Fair* on December 8 reflects the deteriorating situation. Entitled "Brother Jonathan Lame," it shows a bedridden man being tended to by Nurse Columbia and Doctor Disunion. The doctor thinks the man's constitution is so weak that he won't survive without an amputation. "No!" Nurse Columbia pleads, "don't give it up, Doctor." Though the nurse urges that good care can still make an amputation unnecessary, she seems to be implicitly acknowledging the desperate character of the situation.

Events soon confirmed Filmer's judgment. On December 20, South Carolina formally voted to secede from the Union and other states of the Deep South soon followed suit. On January 19, 1861, Stephens published a cartoon in *Vanity Fair* warning the South that secession would eventually bring about

THE RISING OF THE AFRITE.

A NEW APPLICATION OF THE RAREY SYSTEM.

Mr. Rarey Buchanan doesn't see why he can't put the Federal straps on that spunky little colt Miss South Carolina. When he tries to pat her—she bites; when he tries to apply the strap—she kicks. He really doesn't see what is to be done with her—s'poses she'll have to have her own way. To which remark Miss Carolina doesn't say, neigh!

against itself cannot stand," that the South's peculiar institution would slowly wither away.

By February 1861, all the states of the Deep South had seceded from the Union. It was initially President Buchanan's responsibility to react to this situation because President-elect Lincoln did not officially assume office until March 4. Buchanan, however, did next to nothing to counteract the flow of events. He deplored secession, calling it unconstitutional, but blamed the crisis on the North's "intemperate" interference with slavery and argued that there was no constitutional remedy for secession. In his view, the federal government did not have the authority to use coercion to maintain the Union. A

cartoon published in *Frank Leslie's Illustrated* on January 26 mocks Buchanan's weak and contradictory policy. It shows Buchanan attempting to break the wild horse of South Carolina, but when "he tries to pat her—she bites" and when "he tries to apply the strap—she kicks." The key to understanding the cartoon is the reference to "Mr. Raney Buchanan." John S. Raney (1827–1865) was a horse trainer from Ohio who tamed horses by using gentle methods. His fame grew to spectacular proportions. He performed before Queen Victoria, became the subject of sonnets, and even had a waltz composed in his honor. Nonetheless, despite Raney's success with gentle methods, the cartoon implies that a light

PROF. LINCOLN IN HIS GREAT FEAT OF BALANCING.

hand will not work with South Carolina. Raney Buchanan will just have to let the horse go—"To which remark Miss Carolina doesn't say, neigh."

After Lincoln took office, he tried to avoid an immediate confrontation with the seceded states. An impasse quickly arose, however, because Fort Sumter, a federal fort located on an island in Charleston harbor, needed to be re-supplied. If Lincoln sent supplies, the expectation was that the South would resist; if, on the other hand, no supplies were sent, then the troops occupying the fort would have to be withdrawn, which would be a terrible embarrassment for the new administration. Stephens published a cartoon in *Vanity Fair* on March 23 dramatizing Lincoln's predicament. Lincoln is depicted as a circus performer balancing Fort Sumter and peace on his forehead. The caption describes it as Lincoln's "great feat of balancing," a feat that presumably could not last forever. In fact, after weeks of indecision, Lincoln finally ordered the navy to send food to the fort. Acting to preempt this supply effort, the Confederate forces opened fire on April 12. Two days later, Major Robert Anderson, the Northern commander, surrendered. Lincoln called for 75,000 volunteers and Virginia, Tennessee, North Carolina, and Arkansas followed the Deep South into secession. The war that would decide the nature of the American union had begun.

At first, the people of the North thought the war would be over quickly. This delusion was dispelled by the first battle of the war. On July 21, 1861, approximately 30,000 Union forces under the command of Irwin McDowell attacked an equal number of Confederate troops commanded by Pierre G. T. Beauregard at Bull Run, a branch of the Potomac River, about twenty miles south of Washington, D.C., near Manassas Junction, Virginia. Though the battle initially went well for the Northern forces, it ended in a rout of the inexperienced Union army. McDowell's soldiers abandoned their arms and fled back to Washington. Chastened and humbled by this defeat, Northern leaders now realized that preserving the Union was a task that would not be accomplished in a matter of weeks or months. Congress immediately called for a 500,000-member army composed of three-year volunteers and soon thereafter passed an income tax and authorized loans amounting to $140 million. A cartoon published on November 9, 1861, and drawn by Stephens for *Vanity Fair* captures this new sense of Northern resolve. The context of the cartoon is a family quarrel, in which Brother North is about to fight Brother South because the latter has struck Mother Columbia, who is sitting by a table reading the Constitution. Both brothers look determined, but the South, depicted as a son who has physically abused his mother, has obviously been cast in a poor light. "It's time for me to thrash him," Brother North exclaims. "He's got to take it." The cartoon highlights the fratricidal character of the American Civil War and the sort of determination that it took for the North to preserve the Union.

A FAMILY QUARREL, OR THE REASON WHY.

North.—I DID'NT MIND IT, SO LONG AS HE ONLY BULLIED AND THREATENED, BUT WHEN HE STRIKES YOU, MOTHER, I'TS TIME FOR ME TO THRASH HIM—HE'S GOT TO TAKE IT.

Conscription

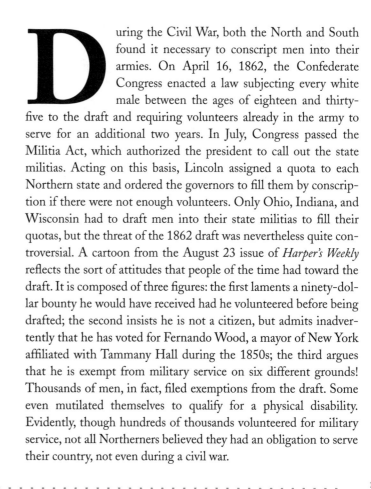

CHAPTER 2

Conscription

During the Civil War, both the North and South found it necessary to conscript men into their armies. On April 16, 1862, the Confederate Congress enacted a law subjecting every white male between the ages of eighteen and thirty-five to the draft and requiring volunteers already in the army to serve for an additional two years. In July, Congress passed the Militia Act, which authorized the president to call out the state militias. Acting on this basis, Lincoln assigned a quota to each Northern state and ordered the governors to fill them by conscription if there were not enough volunteers. Only Ohio, Indiana, and Wisconsin had to draft men into their state militias to fill their quotas, but the threat of the 1862 draft was nevertheless quite controversial. A cartoon from the August 23 issue of *Harper's Weekly* reflects the sort of attitudes that people of the time had toward the draft. It is composed of three figures: the first laments a ninety-dollar bounty he would have received had he volunteered before being drafted; the second insists he is not a citizen, but admits inadvertently that he has voted for Fernando Wood, a mayor of New York affiliated with Tammany Hall during the 1850s; the third argues that he is exempt from military service on six different grounds! Thousands of men, in fact, filed exemptions from the draft. Some even mutilated themselves to qualify for a physical disability. Evidently, though hundreds of thousands volunteered for military service, not all Northerners believed they had an obligation to serve their country, not even during a civil war.

THE DRAFT.

"Och! bad luck to it thin. I've got drafted, and niver a cint for it; and tin days ago I might have volunteered, and got me Ninety Dollars just as aisy as snap yer fingers."

AN EXEMPT.

OFFICER. "You're a Foreigner, you say?"
APPLICANT. "Born in Tipperary, yer honor."
OFFICER. "Did you never get Naturalized?"
APPLICANT. "Ne'er a time."
OFFICER. "Did you never Vote?"
APPLICANT. "Oh! for the matter of votin', yer honor, I allus Votes. Many's the Vote I've guv FERNANDY WOOD; an' av' he were Mayor now———(*is marched off*.)

ABUNDANT DISQUALIFICATION.

"Ugh! How d'you make out that *you* are exempt, eh?"
"I'm over age, I am a Negro, a Minister, a Cripple, a British Subject, and an Habitual Drunkard."

In 1862, a drafted man could avoid military service by paying a substitute to take his place or a three-hundred-dollar fee to the federal government. The latter provision was meant to put a cap on the market price of a substitute, thereby easing the perception that only the wealthy could escape the draft. Despite the cap, the slogan that it was "a rich man's war and a poor man's fight" had wide currency. Three hundred dollars amounted to more than a half a year's salary for a working man during the early 1860s—a large sum to raise on short notice. A cartoon that appeared in *Vanity Fair* on September 6, 1862, mirrors the frustration of those who didn't have the money to avoid the draft: a rich young dandy standing near a military camp tells a man who appears to be a cavalryman already in service that the draft is a "dreadful bore." The system of bounties offered to volunteers by federal, state, and local govern-

ments also encouraged poor men to join the army. In 1862, a volunteer could expect to collect up to five hundred dollars in bounties; in 1864, one thousand dollars. For this kind of money, daring individuals played the dangerous game of enlisting, collecting the bounties, deserting, and then repeating the process all over again.

In 1862, most Northern states excluded free blacks from militia service and the Lincoln administration generally refused to allow African Americans into the federal army. On July 26, 1862, *Vanity Fair* ran a cartoon drawn by Henry Louis Stephens that misleadingly commented on the racial aspects of the draft. The cartoon depicts a nattily dressed black man preferring his "cold" draft to that of the white man's. The insinuation is that blacks wanted to take life easy and let white men do the fighting. Caught in a vicious circle of racial prejudice, Northern

THE NEW "SOCIAL EVIL."

Small Swell.—"DWEADFUL BOAW, THIS DWAFT. DWAGS A FELLAH FWOM THE BOOZUM OF HIS CLUB!"

DRAFTS.

Gentleman of Color.—"Yah! yah! Darkey hab de best ob it now. Dar's de white man's draff, and here's de niggah's!"

BLACK DRAFT.

Colored Person.—"Doctor Andrew's complums, Massa; and he says you must swaller dis here stuff."
Uncle Sam.—"Ugh! take the nasty thing away! I'm sick enough already!"

blacks in 1862 were both barred from the military and unjustly mocked for not being willing to fight for themselves.

Another cartoon lampoons John A. Andrew, the governor of Massachusetts who urged Lincoln to let black units into the federal army. "Doctor Andrew" has prescribed a "black draught," but Uncle Sam refuses to taste it because he thinks it would make his condition worse. Sensitive to the strong feelings of many Democrats living in border states, the War Department kept African Americans out of the federal army until Lincoln issued the final emancipation proclamation on January 1, 1863. Besides freeing all slaves in areas of the Union under rebel control, the proclamation declared that freed black men would be "received into the armed service of the United States,

to garrison forts, positions, stations, and other places, and to man vessels of all sorts in said service." In late January, Lincoln authorized Governor Andrew to organize the "54th Massachusetts"—the all-black but white-officered regiment whose bravery in the face of fire at Fort Wagner was memorialized in the motion picture *Glory*. Other black units took part in the reoccupation of Jacksonville, Florida, and fought ferociously at Milliken's Bend on the Mississippi River. By the end of the war, approximately 200,000 blacks, about 10 percent of the total number of Northern soldiers, served in the Union army.

Since excluding African Americans from the army increased the chances that Northern whites would be drafted, the North's insatiable need for manpower helped to erode the opposition to having blacks in the federal army. Taking black volunteers, however, did not put an end to Northern conscription. On March 3, 1863, Congress departed from its past reliance on state militias and enacted a national draft. Federal officers would register men for the draft, hold lotteries, and induct eligible conscripts into

THE NAUGHTY BOY GOTHAM, WHO WOULD NOT TAKE THE DRAFT.

MAMMY LINCOLN—"*There now, you bad boy, acting that way, when your little sister Penn takes hers like a lady!*"

service. When the law was implemented later that summer, it met with fierce resistance. Disturbances broke out in Boston and Albany and Rochester, New York, and dozens of federal draft officials were killed. In July, New York City had perhaps the worst riot in the nation's history. Hundreds of people were killed, including a number of blacks who were hanged or beaten to death. Looting was rampant and property damage was in the millions of dollars. The tragic event is portrayed in a cartoon that appeared in *Frank Leslie's Illustrated Weekly* on August 29, 1863, after thousands of Northern troops had arrived in the city, restored order, and enforced the draft. An Irish baby in a tantrum (many of the rioters were recent Irish immigrants) refuses to take a "draft" of medicine even though his "little sister Penn[sylvania] takes hers like a lady."

In part because persons arrested by Lincoln's War Department for resisting the draft had no access to courts while the writ of habeas corpus was suspended, no case testing the constitutionality of the draft ever made it to the Supreme Court during the Civil War. However, in preparation for such a case, Chief Justice Roger B. Taney wrote an unpublished memorandum arguing forcefully that Congress's power to "raise and support Armies" did not include the power to conscript troops. A court that did review the constitutionality of the federal draft law was the Pennsylvania Supreme Court, which decided against its constitutionality on November 9, 1863, but soon thereafter reversed itself. In the first decision, three Democratic justices, largely on the ground that national conscription hampered the ability of states to maintain their separate militias, held that the 1863 draft law was unconstitutional. The two Republican justices dissented. After Democratic Chief Justice Walter H. Lowrie's term had expired, Republican Daniel Agnew was elected to the position. A month later, on January 16, 1864, the new Republican majority upheld the constitutionality of the draft law and the two Democratic justices dis-

sented. The opinions and dissents issued in these decisions, as well as the quick reversal itself, underline the draft's controversial character during the Civil War.

Only 46,000 (2 percent) of the 2,100,000 men who served in the Northern army were drafted into service. Although an additional 118,000 of the total were substitutes whom drafted men had paid to avoid serving in the army, the vast majority of the Union army—nearly 92 percent—was composed of volunteers. Patriotism, of course, inclined many to volunteer, but those subject to the draft could collect bounties from federal, state, and local governments if they enlisted first. In this sense, the draft aided the North's efforts to field an army capable of defeating the South.

The Supreme Court did not consider the constitutionality of conscription until *Arver v. United States,* which came before the high court in 1918, the last year of World War I. By this time the question was no longer controversial. The Court unanimously upheld the draft law's constitutionality, rejecting the argument that state authority over the militia precluded national conscription. The power "to raise and support armies" was clearly delegated to Congress and that power was "supreme." A week later, in *Goldman v. United States* and *Ruthenberg v. United States,* the Court, again unanimously, upheld criminal convictions of persons who had conspired to violate the draft law or encouraged others not to register for the draft. A 1920 cartoon that appeared in *Stars and Stripes* suggests that the unanimity of the Court mirrored an emerging social consensus. A draft dodger, the cartoon declares, will have to carry a ball and chain of public opprobrium even after he gets out of jail in six months. Though the Supreme Court's 1918 decisions did not quiet all controversy about the draft during World War I, they strongly supported the conclusion that Congress had indeed acted within its constitutional powers when it first drafted men during the Civil War.

It'll take longer to lose the ball!

EMANCIPATIO

The Thirteenth Amendment

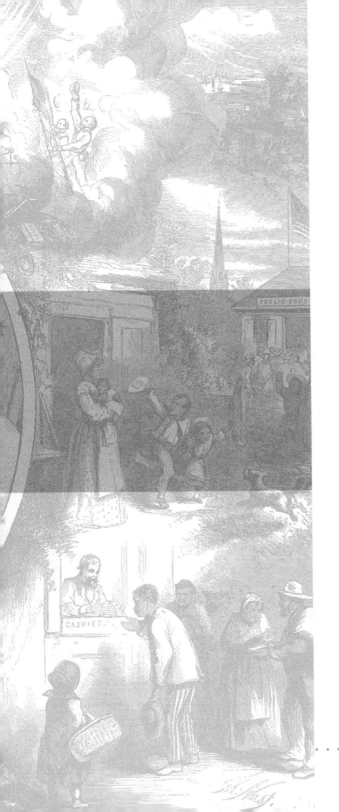

CHAPTER 3

The Thirteenth Amendment
Abolition of Slavery

A movement to abolish slavery in the United States arose during the first half of the nineteenth century. In 1831, William Lloyd Garrison of Massachusetts established an abolitionist paper, *The Liberator,* and organized the New England Anti-Slavery Society. Two years later, he and other abolitionists founded the American Anti-Slavery Society. Because the Constitution implicitly recognized slavery, Garrison called it "an agreement with hell" and demanded immediate total emancipation. Other abolitionists were more moderate in tone, but Southern states did not distinguish among the various strains of abolitionism. They banned abolitionist literature from Southern post offices and punished anyone who criticized slavery. Under these conditions, abolitionism disappeared in the South, but grew steadily in the North, forming a key constituency of the emerging Republican Party in the 1850s. By this time, members of anti-slavery societies and their sympathizers, though still in the minority, numbered in the hundreds of thousands.

Abolitionists played a significant part in the events leading up to the Civil War. Some of their number violated the federal Fugitive Slave Act by resisting the efforts of Southern slave owners to take their runaways back to slavery in the South. Others shipped arms to people fighting to keep slavery out of "Bleeding Kansas" or helped finance John Brown's attack in October 1859 on Harper's Ferry—a small Virginia town on the Potomac River northwest of Washington. Hoping to arm the slaves of the countryside, establish a Negro Republic, and then make war on the Southern states,

A PREMATURE MOVEMENT.

JOHN BROWN. "Here! Take this, and follow me. My name's Brown."

Brown seized a federal arsenal. Though he and his eighteen followers occupied the arsenal for two days, no slave revolt took place. Ridiculing this effort to win freedom for the slaves, a cartoon of the time pictures a black man who refuses to follow Brown because he is too busy planting crops on his master's plantation. The cartoon would have appealed to those Northerners who perceived abolitionism as a completely unrealistic objective in the late 1850s. On December 2, 1859, Brown was hanged for treason, conspiracy, and murder, but he quickly became a martyr to the growing abolitionist movement and a song bearing his name and commemorating his ideals quickly became popular.

On March 2, 1861, just two days before Abraham Lincoln took office, President James Buchanan signed a proposed Thirteenth Amendment to the Constitution of the United States, thereby submitting the measure to the states for ratification. The proposed amendment read:

> *"No amendment shall be made to the Constitution which will authorize or give to Congress the power to abolish or interfere, within any State, with the domestic institutions thereof, including that of persons held to labor or service by the laws of said State."*

Because the states in the Deep South had already seceded and several Northern state legislatures were controlled by the Republican Party, this attempt to restore the Union on terms the South could accept was a complete failure. The irony is that its demise left room in the Constitution for a different Thirteenth Amendment that would have an opposite effect.

At the beginning of the Civil War, abolitionism was not popular in many areas of the North. A cartoon published by Henry Louis Stephens in *Vanity Fair* on May 17, 1862, reflects this anti-abolitionist

"I SHALL PUSH THE ENEMY TO THE WALL."

(General McClellan's Dispatch of 4th May.)

The Monotonous Minstrel.

President Lincoln, (to *H. G.*)—"Go away, you tiresome vagrant! It's always the same old croak-ing tune, 'Abolition, Abolition, Marching On!'"

sentiment. It portrays abolitionism as a ball and chain attached to the foot of General George B. McClellan's effort to push the enemy of secession to the wall. Since the South would never rejoin the Union if the North favored emancipating the slaves, abolitionism was perceived to be a hindrance to the war effort and an obstacle to restoring the Union.

Though he personally detested slavery, Abraham Lincoln kept his distance from the abolitionists and the Radical Republicans, a formidable political force in Congress led by two dedicated abolitionists: Charles Sumner in the Senate and Thaddeus Stevens in the House of Representatives. Not want-ing to get too far ahead of public opinion, Lincoln did every-thing he could during the first year and a half of hostilities not to alienate the border states, the pro-war elements of the Democratic Party, and the pro-slavery soldiers serving in the Northern armies. He repeatedly insisted that restoring the Union, not ending slavery in the Southern states, was the war's primary purpose. A cartoon by Stephens appearing in *Vanity Fair* on September 15, 1862, expresses this theme. Horace Greeley, the editor of the influential *New York Tribune* and a prominent abolitionist, is portrayed as a "tiresome vagrant" who Lincoln sends away.

WHAT WILL HE DO WITH THEM?

A. L.—"Darn these here blackbirds!—if nobody won't buy 'em I'll have to open the cages and let 'em fly!"

Perhaps reflecting evolving public opinion, Congress slowly moved closer to abolitionism during 1862. In April, it abolished slavery in the District of Columbia and, two months later, in all federal territories. In the first instance, the federal government paid compensation to the owners, but not in the second. In July, Congress enacted the second Confiscation Act, which provided that slaves of rebels who came within Union lines should be deemed captives and forever free. Though Lincoln did little to enforce this provision of the Confiscation Act, he prepared the public for the eventual emancipation of the slaves by urging the border slave states to buy slaves from their owners and receive compensation from the federal government. No border state accepted Lincoln's offer, which is the underlying meaning of a cartoon entitled "What Will He Do With Them." Presumably drawn by Stephens, the cartoon suggests that Lincoln would in the end have to free the slaves living in the border states if Congress and the states did not implement a plan of gradual compensated emancipation. The cartoon appeared in *Vanity Fair* on October 4, 1862, just a couple of weeks after Lincoln issued the preliminary Emancipation Proclamation, which declared that all slaves held in areas still in rebellion on January 1, 1863, would be free immediately and forever.

It is arguable that another cartoon describes the preliminary Emancipation Proclamation as Lincoln's "last warning" to the South. Appearing in *Harper's Weekly* on October 11, 1862, it depicts Lincoln ready to chop down the tree of slavery in which the Southern states are hiding. As slavery was the economic foundation of the Confederacy's war effort, Lincoln claimed he had the constitutional authority as the commander and chief of the armed forces to abolish it for the purpose of quelling the rebellion and restoring the Union. His critics claimed

LINCOLN'S LAST WARNING.
"Now, if you don't come down, I'll cut the Tree *from under you*."

LATEST FROM ETHIOPIA.

Tom.—"'Say, Pomp, a 'liable darkey tell me just now dat Jeff Davis gwine to talliate 'bout de President's proclamation—he gwine to declare all de niggers in de Norf States slaves arter de fust ob Janwery next."

Pomp.—" Bress us all !"

that neither international nor military law sanctioned such a confiscation of private property. The market value of the millions of slaves that were freed by the Emancipation Proclamation was in the billions of dollars. Never before or since has a president on his own authority taken away so much "property" from so many American citizens.

The Emancipation Proclamation freed only the slaves who were under the control of the Confederate armies. It did nothing for the slaves living in border states or in those areas of Southern states already occupied by Northern armies. In short, it gave freedom to slaves who were not within Lincoln's control and refused it to those who were. A cartoon by Howard Del (a pen name for J. H. Howard), published in *Vanity Fair* on October 25, 1862, indirectly comments on this odd result. It shows a black man at an oyster bar reporting to his friend a rumor that Jefferson Davis, the president of the Confederate States, had issued a proclamation enslaving all Northern free blacks as of January 1, 1863, the very day Lincoln's Emancipation Proclamation was to take effect. His surprised friend replies, "Bress us all!"

Two other cartoons represent contrasting styles and points of view. The first, published in *Vanity Fair* on December 27, 1862, darkly intimates that African Americans would not, despite their "new situation," be able to escape from their subordinate status in American life. The second, drawn by Thomas Nast and published in *Harper's Weekly* on January 24, 1863, celebrates emancipation. Family life, industry, and public education will replace all the past cruelties that the slaves had had to endure for centuries.

To achieve total emancipation and abolish slavery permanently, the Radical Republicans proposed the Thirteenth Amendment to Congress in early 1864. The Senate adopted it on April 8, 1864, a year before Confederate General Robert E. Lee surrendered to General Ulysses S. Grant at Appomattox

Open
Jan 1st
1863

Closed
Dec 31st
1862

BOBBETT-HOOPER

THE NEW PLACE.

Inevitable Contraband.—"YAH! YAH! DIS CHILE'S ON DE MOVE TO HIS NEW SITUMAVATION.   WONDER WHAT SORT OF PUSSON NEW MASSA'S GWINE TO BE!"

THE EMANCIPATION OF THE NEGROES, JANUARY, 1863—THE PAST AND THE FUTURE—Drawn by Mr. Thomas Nast.

Court House. The House of Representatives could not achieve the required two-thirds majority vote until January 31, 1865. On February 26, a cartoon appeared in *Frank Leslie's Illustrated Newspaper* depicting the amendment as a dream that had come true for Lincoln in the form of a valentine. Perhaps the cartoonist was indirectly poking fun at Lincoln's well-documented belief in the power and significance of dreams. In any case, several weeks after this cartoon appeared, Lincoln was assassinated, fulfilling one of the president's own darkest premonitions.

Before the Thirteenth Amendment could become a part of the Constitution, three-quarters of the states, twenty-seven of the thirty-six then in the Union, had to ratify the amendment. On December 18, 1865, ratification was deemed achieved even though some of the ratifying states were provisional Southern governments formed under President Andrew Johnson's plan for reconstituting lawful government in the South. Controlled by Radical Republicans, Congress refused to recognize these governments or seat their representatives, yet counted their votes in favor of the Thirteenth Amendment. A number of additional states subsequently ratified the amendment, which eliminated any concern for the legal status of emancipation. Today the legitimacy of the Thirteenth Amendment is unquestioned.

UNCLE ABE'S VALENTINE SENT BY COLUMBIA.

AN ENVELOPE FULL OF BROKEN CHAINS.

CHAPTER 4

The Fourteenth Amendment

The Fourteenth Amendment

Due Process and Equal Protection

After President Abraham Lincoln was assassinated in April 1865, his successor, Andrew Johnson, pursued a relatively lenient Southern reconstruction policy by pardoning rebels who took a loyalty oath and supported the Thirteenth Amendment. These Southerners were allowed to elect delegates to state constitutional conventions. These conventions abolished slavery and provided for the election of state officers, including state legislatures. By the end of 1865, Johnson's reconstruction policy was nearly implemented. Many of the newly created Southern state legislatures had ratified the Thirteenth Amendment, appointed senators to serve in Congress (before the Seventeenth Amendment was ratified in 1913, state legislatures chose United States senators), and scheduled congressional elections.

When it convened in December 1865, Congress, led by the Radical Republicans, refused the representatives of the Southern states their seats in the Senate and the House, thereby blocking Johnson's effort to restore the Southern states to the Union. The Radicals acted for reasons of both principle and expediency. Johnson's lenient approach to reconstruction did nothing to stop the new Southern legislatures from enacting so-called black codes that imposed severe legal disabilities on the former slaves. The fact that these same states had elected to the Senate and the House dozens of men who had served in the Confederate Congress was an additional concern. The Radicals also feared that a reconstructed South would ally itself with Northern Democrats and

THE CRUEL UNCLE AND THE VETOED BABES IN THE WOOD.

wrest control of both houses of Congress from the Republican Party. The likelihood of this scenario was especially true in regard to the House of Representatives because the abolition of slavery meant that an African American in the South would no longer, for purposes of calculating representation, be counted as three-fifths of a person. After the 1870 census, the number of seats in the House representing former slave states would go up, even if these same states denied the newly freed slaves the right to vote.

Dominated as it was by Northern states and Radical Republicans, Congress passed the Freedmen's Bureau Bill on February 19, 1866, and the Civil Rights Bill on March 13. The first bill extended the life of the Freedmen's Bureau, a wartime relief agency for the newly freed slaves. The second bill was a more elaborate effort to protect the civil rights of African Americans in the South. It granted United States citizenship to the former slaves and delineated their basic civil rights. They had the right "to sue, be parties, and give evidence, to inherit, purchase, lease, sell, hold, and convey real and personal property." In addition, each had the "full and equal benefit of all laws and proceedings for the security of person and property, as is enjoyed by white citizens." Johnson reacted to these congressional initiatives by vetoing both bills, an event that became the focal point of a cartoon published in *Frank Leslie's Illustrated Newspaper* on May 12, 1866. A "cruel uncle" is pictured taking a white and a black child out to Veto Wood to shoot them with the pistol he carries in his belt. Johnson justified his vetoes on the ground that both bills were unconstitutional intrusions of the federal government into civil rights, an area that had traditionally been reserved to the states.

Though the Freedmen's Bureau Bill died quietly, Congress enacted the Civil Rights Bill over Johnson's veto on April 9, 1866. To overcome Johnson's constitutional objection to this law, the Joint Committee on Reconstruction on April 30 proposed what later became the Fourteenth Amendment. Section I of the proposed amendment defined national citizenship ("All persons born or naturalized in the United States, and subject to the jurisdiction thereof, are citizens of the United States and of the State wherein they reside.") and authorized in general terms federal protection of basic civil rights against state interference:

> No State shall make or enforce any law which shall abridge the privileges or immunities of citizens of the United States; nor shall any State deprive any person of life, liberty, or property, without due process of law; nor deny to any person within its jurisdiction the equal protection of the laws.

If ratified by three-quarters of the states, this language of the Fourteenth Amendment would insure the constitutionality of the Civil Rights Act. The "black codes" that discriminated against African Americans would thereby become invalid, and the federal government would have clear authority to protect the more specific rights enumerated in the act.

Congress passed the final version of the Fourteenth Amendment on June 13, 1866. At this point, however, the Republicans confronted a major dilemma: the Fourteenth Amendment could not be ratified without the help of the Southern states. A cartoon published in *Frank Leslie's Illustrated Newspaper* possibly hints at the problem. Mother Columbia admonishes Andrew Johnson to fix the family kettle so that she can use it to feed her young toddler—the Fourteenth Amendment. The holes in the kettle of "The Reconstructed South"

MENDING THE FAMILY KETTLE.

Columbia—" *Now, Andy, I wish you and your boys would hurry up that job, because I want to use that kettle right away. You are all talking too much about it.*"

had to be plugged before the Fourteenth Amendment could be ratified.

The Radical Republicans resolved their dilemma by making ratification of the Fourteenth Amendment a condition for readmission to the Union. Congress would seat Southern representatives only if their states had ratified an amendment that subordinated their racial policies to federal supervision. At first, only Tennessee was willing to accept this deal. Ten Southern states rejected the amendment, placing their hopes on the upcoming November congressional elections. If the Northern electorate turned against the Radical Republicans in favor of Johnson's more lenient reconstruction policies, the Southern states would perhaps be able to rejoin the Union without losing significant control of their racial policies.

The election, however, dashed Southern hopes. Obtaining more than a two-thirds majority in both houses, the Republicans won a huge victory. Relying upon this mandate, they initiated a more radical program of reconstruction by enacting, over Johnson's veto, the Military Reconstruction Acts of 1867 and 1868. Bypassing the governments that had been created the year before under Johnson's plan, these laws imposed a system of military rule on the South (excepting Tennessee) by dividing the rebel states into five military districts. A cartoon by Thomas Nast in *Harper's Weekly* illuminates one reason why so many Republicans of the time turned toward a more radical and harsh program of Southern reconstruction. It seemed to them, based on news reports from the South, that Southern justice had degenerated into a system that terrorized African Americans and Northerners alike.

The Military Reconstruction Acts permitted each Southern state to initiate a process of ending military rule by calling a constitutional convention, but these same acts also disfranchised many former rebels and enfranchised all the former slaves. The same electorate had to ratify the new state constitution before it could be sent to Congress for its approval. Once Congress approved the new constitution, the state would become entitled to representation in Congress if the legislature, elected under the new constitution, ratified the Fourteenth Amendment. Military rule of the South would end when the Fourteenth Amendment had been ratified by the requisite three-quarters of the states.

Two cartoons that appeared in 1867 reveal the attitudes of Northern Republicans. On April 13, soon after Congress overrode Johnson's veto of the first Military Reconstruction Act, Thomas Nast drew a cartoon for *Harper's Weekly* that pictures a jubilant black man on his way to the polls and a sulking ex-confederate with no place to go. The caption proclaims "We Accept The Situation." Two months later, on July 13, in *Frank Leslie's Illustrated Newspaper*, a cartoon portrays a stern Dr. Congress giving a little girl her "reconstruction dose" while "Mrs. Columbia" admonishes Johnson not to interfere. Both cartoons indicate the North's support for the Fourteenth Amendment and the tough reconstruction policy of the Radical Republicans.

During the fall of 1867, all ten Southern states still outside the Union voted to call constitutional

"WE ACCEPT THE SITUATION."

THE RECONSTRUCTION DOSE.

NAUGHTY ANDY—"*Don't take that physic, Sis, it's nasty—kick his shins.*"
MRS. COLUMBIA—"*My dear Andy, don't be a bad boy, don't interfere—Dr. Congress knows what's best for Sissy.*"

conventions that met during the following winter and spring. These conventions supported black suffrage and the disfranchisement of a large percentage of the white population. State legislatures elected under new state constitutions quickly ratified the Fourteenth Amendment. A cartoon that appeared on March 21, 1868, in *Harpers Weekly* symbolizes what impact the amendment was having on Johnson's reputation. A "little boy" who is handling books "above his capacity" picks out volume fourteen, falls, and is crushed under its weight. Johnson had campaigned against the Amendment during the 1866 elections and had vetoed the Reconstruction Acts of 1867. In March 1868, the Republicans in the House of Representatives impeached Johnson, claiming that his firing of Secretary of War Edwin Stanton violated the Office of Tenure Act. Though the Senate failed by one vote to convict Johnson and remove him from office, his political career, as the cartoon implies, was over. Later that year, the Democratic National Convention nominated Horatio Seymour, not Johnson, to run against General Ulysses S. Grant, the Republican nominee who won the presidential election in November.

By June 1868, three-quarters of the states had ratified the amendment, including seven Southern states: Alabama, Arkansas, North Carolina, South Carolina, Georgia, Florida, and Louisiana. The Fourteenth Amendment, however, was not proclaimed to be a part of the Constitution until July 28, 1868, a month after Congress had granted these states representation in Congress and formally readmitted them into the Union. Perhaps the delay was to soften the irony of the situation. States outside the Union had taken part in the Union's constitutional ratification process as a condition to rejoin that same Union. ⚖

THIS LITTLE BOY WOULD PERSIST IN HANDLING BOOKS ABOVE
HIS CAPACITY.

AND THIS WAS THE DISASTROUS RESULT.

The Fifteenth
Amendment

CHAPTER 5

The Fifteenth Amendment
Voting Rights

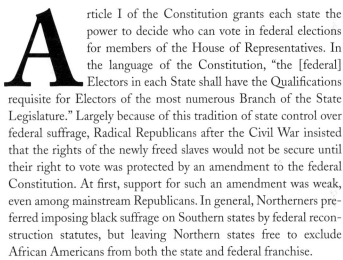

Article I of the Constitution grants each state the power to decide who can vote in federal elections for members of the House of Representatives. In the language of the Constitution, "the [federal] Electors in each State shall have the Qualifications requisite for Electors of the most numerous Branch of the State Legislature." Largely because of this tradition of state control over federal suffrage, Radical Republicans after the Civil War insisted that the rights of the newly freed slaves would not be secure until their right to vote was protected by an amendment to the federal Constitution. At first, support for such an amendment was weak, even among mainstream Republicans. In general, Northerners preferred imposing black suffrage on Southern states by federal reconstruction statutes, but leaving Northern states free to exclude African Americans from both the state and federal franchise.

At the time of his death in 1865, Abraham Lincoln's policy on black suffrage was cautious. "I would myself prefer," he wrote, "that [the vote] were now conferred on the very intelligent, and on those who served our cause as soldiers." On August 5, 1865, a cartoon by Thomas Nast appeared in *Harper's Weekly* that articulated the rhetorical force of Lincoln's latter point. It shows Columbia asking herself if she can entrust the franchise to former rebels with pardons if she can't entrust the same to a black soldier who had lost his leg fighting for the Union. The clear implication of the cartoon was that the African Americans who fought for the Union should have the right to vote.

PARDON.

Columbia.—"Shall I Trust These Men,

FRANCHISE.

And Not This Man?"

After the elections of 1866, the Republicans enacted reconstruction statutes that gave the vote to black former slaves living in Southern states but disfranchised many of the white former rebels. Under these conditions, former slave owners running for office often had to seek out the black vote. Such a radical reversal of roles posed an easy target for Northern cartoonists. For example, in a cartoon published on April 6, 1867, in *Harper's Weekly* and entitled "The New Era," former Confederate General Wade Hampton from South Carolina, pictured with exaggerated spurs and his riding whip, is shown inviting an "influential colored voter" to dinner. Prior to the Civil War, Hampton was one of the richest planters in the South and, following it, one of the most important white politicians in South Carolina. The black voter declines Hampton's invitation, informing him that he has already promised "to *sleep* with Massa Pinckney." The Pinckney family was one of the oldest and most prestigious families in South Carolina, having had two of its members, Charles Cotesworth Pinckney and Charles Pinckney, attend the Constitutional Convention in 1787. Ironically, it was the former Pinckney who had made the suggestion that slaves should count as three-fifths of a person for purposes of calculating representation in the House of Representatives.

An unprecedented level of racial violence marred the elections of 1868, particularly in Southern states. The Ku Klux Klan, founded in Tennessee in 1866, unleashed a campaign of violence and intimidation throughout the south against Republican leaders of both races. Marauding whites disrupted Republican campaign events, assaulting and killing black leaders, all in an effort to put an end to black suffrage and restore white man's government. What can only be described as massacres were not uncommon. In one such incident, two hundred blacks were killed. In a cartoon published in *Harper's Weekly* on October 3, 1868, Thomas Nast, a staunch Republican, memorialized the temper of the times and delineated what was at stake in the upcoming elections. In the background, the Democratic presidential nominee, Horatio Seymour, a former governor of New York who had called New York City draft rioters "his friends" after they had killed dozens of blacks in 1863, and Frank Blair of Missouri, his running mate, are grouped with a number of former Confederate generals, including Robert E. Lee and Nathan B. Forrest. All are pictured with swords and guns drawn. In the foreground, a black man, "the modern Samson," has just had his hair shorn by a woman, "Southern Democracy," using the razor of "the lost cause regained." The cartoon echoes the violence of the times and implicitly hints that the future of African Americans would be bleak if they lost their right to vote in state and federal elections.

THE NEW ERA.

GENERAL WADE HAMPTON (*to influential colored voter*). "Of course you'll *Dine* with me on Thursday?"

COLORED VOTER. "Not on Phursday, Massa HAMPTON. On Phursday I'se promised to *Sleep* with Massa PINCKNEY."

The Modern Samson.

Although Ulysses S. Grant defeated Seymour in the presidential election of 1868 by winning seventy-three percent of the electoral votes, he won only fifty-two percent of the popular vote. Republicans feared that the thin margin of victory was an indication of an ominous trend and that the Democratic party could soon be in control of congress and many state legislatures. In part to regain the electoral advantage, the Republicans proposed the Fifteenth Amendment, which Congress passed on February 26, 1868. The Republicans could have proposed a positive amendment, one that would have guaranteed the right to vote in federal elections to all males over twenty-one years of age. Instead they took a more negative and conservative course:

> The right of citizens of the United States to vote shall not be denied or abridged by the United States or by any State on account of race, color, or previous condition of servitude.

This language barred the states and the federal government from engaging in racial discrimination in voting, but it did not take from the states their general control over the right to vote. States would yet be able to establish non-racial qualifications for the right to vote, such as property or literacy qualifications. Those Radical Republicans who perhaps would have preferred a broader amendment consoled themselves with the fact that the proposed amendment would not invalidate the provisions of the reconstruction statutes that denied former rebels the right to vote.

For the rest of 1869 and part of 1870, the Republican and Democratic parties fought over the ratification of the Fifteenth Amendment state by state. In many Southern states, the results of these contests were somewhat preordained because blacks already had the vote. North Carolina, Louisiana, South Carolina, and Arkansas all ratified the amendment in March 1869. Congress gave Virginia, Texas, and Mississippi an additional incentive to ratify the amendment by making it a precondition for these unreconstructed states to rejoin the Union. Struggles over ratification were especially fierce in states where the par-

FIRST NEWSBOY—" Say, Bill, who's that?"
SECOND DITTO—" That! why, that there chap are the Fifteenth Amendment."

ties were equally divided and the future black vote could possibly control the balance of power. With an estimated ten thousand black residents, New York's ratification process was especially protracted. On April 14, 1869, the New York legislature ratified the amendment, but on January 5, 1870, it passed a resolution withdrawing its consent to it—an action that the state did not formally rescind until March 30, 1970. A series of cartoons published in *Frank Leslie's Illustrated Newspaper* by E. S. Bisbee provide some insight into the situation. The first, which appeared on January 1, 1870, pictures an African American as the new "big man on the block"; the second, on June 4, 1870, after the amendment had been ratified by the requisite three-quarters of the states, parodies how the New York Democratic Party must "cultivate" the black vote; the third, on November 12, 1870, depicts a black man about to go to sleep on "election eve" asking his mother, Horace Greeley, the powerful but erratic

CULTIVATING SAMBO.

GRAND DEMOCRATIC CHORUS —" An, faith, it's little we knew how valuable it was till it blossomed."

AN ELECTION IDYL—[*After Tennyson.*]

You must wake and call me early, call me early, mother dear,
To morrow 'll be the happiest day of all the glad New Year.

editor of the *Herald Tribune,* to wake him early so that he can cast his vote for the first time.

The Fifteenth Amendment was formally ratified on March 30, 1870. It was regarded by many Republicans as an important step in achieving legal and political equality for African Americans. Later events, however, worked to erode much of the amendment's significance. Groups such as the Ku Klux Klan and the White League continued to deprive blacks of their right to vote throughout the Southern states. A cartoon published on October 31, 1874, in *Harper's Weekly* satirizes the confident prediction of Southern newspapers that Democrats would be victorious in the upcoming elections. It shows whites casting their ballots at "The Immaculate White Man's Polls," while a hard-looking Southern gentleman, holding a pistol, stares down blacks holding their Republican tickets at a window. The cartoon implied that Southern Democratic victories were only achieved through the intimidation of black voters. After the Northern armies were withdrawn from the South following the disputed Hayes-Tilden election of 1876, the situation deteriorated even further. Northern Republicans became indifferent to the plight of blacks in the South, and the federal government failed in its duty to protect their right to vote. Black voting was suppressed in Southern and certain border states until Congress enacted the Voting Rights Act of 1965—a full ninety-five years after the Fifteenth Amendment was ratified. 📖

"EVERY THING POINTS TO A DEMOCRATIC VICTORY THIS FALL."—Southern Papers.

The Sixteenth Amendment

CHAPTER 6

The Sixteenth Amendment

Federal Taxation

Supreme Court decisions interpreting the Constitution can be overturned by a later decision or by a constitutional amendment. For an amendment to become a part of the Constitution, it must gain the approval of two-thirds of both houses of Congress and three-fourths of the states must ratify it. Only a handful of Supreme Court decisions have been reversed through this long and cumbersome process. The Eleventh Amendment (1795), which made states immune from civil suits in federal courts, overturned *Chisholm v. Georgia* (1793); and the Thirteenth and Fourteenth Amendments, which, respectively, abolished slavery and granted citizenship to all persons "born or naturalized" in the United States, nullified the infamous *Dred Scott* case (1857). The Sixteenth Amendment also negated a Supreme Court decision. In *Pollock v. Farmers' Loan & Trust Co.* (1895), the Court overturned an earlier Supreme Court decision upholding the constitutionality of a federal income tax. Eighteen years later, the Sixteenth Amendment reversed *Pollock* by granting Congress the power "to lay and collect taxes on incomes, from whatever source derived, without apportionment among the several States, and without regard to any census or enumeration." While constitutional amendments that reverse Supreme Court decisions have been relatively rare, the Court itself has often set aside its own decisions, either by directly overruling them or by narrowing their scope.

In 1862, Congress enacted a federal income tax to help pay for the Civil War. William Springer, a lawyer, objected to the tax on the ground that the Constitution said that Congress could not impose a capitation (head) or other "direct tax" unless it was apportioned among the states based on population. Springer argued that the income tax was unconstitutional because it was a "direct tax" keyed to income, not to population. A rich state with a small population would pay more tax than a poor state with a large population. In *Springer v. United States* (1881), the Supreme Court responded to this argument by narrowly defining the category of "direct taxes" to include only head taxes and taxes on land. Income taxes, the Court ruled, were "indirect taxes" that Congress could impose without abiding by the constitutional rule requiring apportionment.

After the Civil War income tax law expired in 1872, Congress did not pass a similar tax until 1894, when agrarian radicals and populist social reformers from the South and West joined Eastern liberals in demanding an income tax to balance the budget and alleviate economic disparities. Republican conservatives denounced the tax as a dangerous step in the direction of communism. Cartoonists working for New York papers hinted that southern Democrats supported the tax because it would burden the industrialized North more than the agricultural South. One such cartoon, drawn by Victor and published in *Judge* on June 16, 1894, harked back to the Civil War. Beside a woman (the North) lying on the ground with a quill pen protruding from her back, an ex-confederate brigadier general, now a Democratic senator, draped in the robe of a dramatic actor, expresses his willingness to exchange his sword for a pen. The title of the cartoon is "The Democratic Richelieu," a reference to Armand Jean du Plessis, Cardinal and Duke of Richelieu (1585–1642) and longtime chief minister to King Louis XIII. Nicknamed "The Red Eminence," Richelieu dedicated his life to the establishment of royal absolutism in France. He prohibited private warfare, reduced the power of the French nobility, and even prohibited dueling, all of which helped to solidify the power of the French king. In 1839, Edward Bulwer-Lytton, a British politician, poet, playwright, critic and novelist, published a play entitled *Richelieu*. It recounted the deeds and achievements of the seventeenth-century statesman and had wide circulation during the latter half

THE DEMOCRATIC RICHELIEU.

Democratic senator (*ex-confederate brigadier*)—"Take away the sword. States can be ruined without it. Bring me the pen. The pen is mightier than the sword!"

of the nineteenth century. In the play, the lead character remarks, "Beneath the rule of men entirely great, the pen is mightier than the sword.

"Take away the sword—States can be ruined without it!" The second half of the first sentence, now a cliché in regard to the power of the written word, is the punch line of the cartoon's caption. The cartoon artfully denigrates southern Democrats who were supporting the new federal income tax. They were, the cartoon implies, little more than ex-confederates out to "ruin" the United States, not by violence, but by a levy that would drain money and power away from the industrialized North.

Despite the opposition of the Republican Party, a Democratic Congress incorporated a two percent tax on all incomes over four thousand dollars into the Wilson-Gorman Tariff Act of August 15, 1894. Charles Pollock, a stockholder in the Farmers' Loan and Trust Company, sued the bank to enjoin it

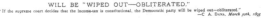

WILL BE "WIPED OUT—OBLITERATED."
" If the supreme court decides that the income-tax is constitutional, the Democratic party will be wiped out—obliterated."
—C. A. DANA, *March 30th, 1895.*

THE LATEST UNFORTUNATE EDITION OF AN UNFORTUNATE ANIMAL

from paying the tax. The case was clearly collusive since both parties wanted the same result: a judicial ruling that the tax was unconstitutional. Though the Supreme Court normally refuses to hear collusive suits, it agreed to hear the case on an expedited basis, a clear indication of the political intensity surrounding the income tax question.

With Justice Howell Jackson absent, the Court heard arguments in early March 1895 and handed down its decision on April 8. The decision was in three parts. In regard to income from state and municipal bonds, the Court unanimously ruled that the law was an unconstitutional tax on the states themselves. Second, in a vote of 6 to 2, the Court decided that a tax on income from real property was a direct tax. Accordingly, the federal government could not constitutionally collect tax on rental income unless it was allocated in proportion to the populations of the various states. On the last but crucial issue of the case—

was the tax on private and corporate incomes a direct tax?—the Court split 4 to 4. Since a tie vote at the Supreme Court leaves the lower court's decision standing, the result was that the main provisions of the 1894 income tax law remained in effect.

Two cartoons that appeared in New York weeklies indirectly reflect the unpopularity of the Supreme Court's decision in *Pollock,* at least in the industrialized Northeast. In one by Victor, published in *Judge* on April 27, Charles A. Dana, the respected editor of the New York *Sun,* is quoted as saying that the Democratic Party would be "obliterated" if the Supreme Court upheld the income tax law. With the Supreme Court decision at her feet, Columbia finds the Democratic donkey hiding sheepishly under the Capitol's dome. The cartoon seems to suggest that Dana's prediction will come true unless the Democratic Party withdraws its support for the income tax law. In the second cartoon—drawn by J. S. Pughe and which

WITHOUT A FRIEND.

appeared in *Puck*—the donkey in the upper left-hand corner, laboring under the heavy load of the income tax law, expects help from the Supreme Court. The Court's decision, however, leaves the donkey "high and dry."

In part because of the popular dissatisfaction with the *Pollock* decision, but probably more so because of the inconclusive nature of the 4 to 4 decision, the Supreme Court immediately scheduled a rehearing of the case. With all the justices present, the Court heard argument for three days in early May. A week later a cartoon entitled "Without A Friend" by Pughe again appeared in *Puck*. The income tax law is pictured as a mongrel dog with the Supreme Court's decision (a tin can) tied to its tail. Perhaps Pughe is suggesting that the Court's earlier split decision increased the public's hostility to the income tax law.

On May 20, 1895, the Court handed down a decision overturning *Springer* and invalidating the entire 1894 tax law on the ground that it was a "direct tax" that had to be apportioned in accordance with the respective populations of the states. The vote was 5 to 4, but, surprisingly, Justice Jackson, who had been absent from the first *Pollock* decision, was not the fifth vote against the tax law. One of the justices who had initially voted in favor of the law switched sides, which shows that individual justices can change their minds, just as the Court itself can. What is perhaps more troubling is that the Sixteenth Amendment became necessary only because a single justice flip-flopped on the issue of the tax's constitutionality.

Another cartoon by Victor entitled "Crowned 'King of Blunderers'" appeared a couple of weeks after the Supreme Court handed down its second *Pollock* decision. It depicts Chief Justice Melville W. Fuller, author of the Court's majority opinion in the case, placing a dunce cap on the head of

CROWNED "KING OF BLUNDERERS."

"It was the most foolish thing the Democratic party ever did—and it has done a great many foolish things—to enact this income-tax. The Supreme Court of the United States is entitled to the thanks of the country for its decision."—D. B. HILL.

Democratic President Grover Cleveland and quotes with approval David Bennett Hill's endorsement of the Court's decision invalidating the tax. Elected in 1892, Cleveland in principle supported a federal income tax, though he had reservations about the timing of the 1894 tax. The views of Hill, the recognized leader of the New York State Democratic Party, though typical of wealthy people living in the Northeast, were not necessarily shared by Democrats living in the South and West.

The income tax litigation stirred popular emotions and feelings during the mid-1890s and convinced many Americans that the Court was on the side of the rich. With the return of prosperity after 1896, however, the issue of a federal income tax fell out of the political limelight. Not until 1906 did income tax bills begin to reappear in Congress, their proponents arguing that the constitutional question should be resubmitted to the Court. Ironically, in 1909, when a Democratic income tax bill stood an excellent chance of becoming law, conservatives in the Republican Party claimed that passage of this apparently unconstitutional law would damage the judiciary and offered in its place a constitutional amendment granting Congress the power to impose an income tax. Liberals supported the measure even though they knew that the purpose of the Republican-sponsored amendment was to kill the income tax law and that conservative Republicans fully expected the amendment would not win the approval of three-fourths of the states. However, on July 12, 1909, the proposed amendment passed both houses by wide margins: 77 to 0 in the Senate; 318 to 14 in the House. And, to the surprise and consternation of the conservative Republicans, the requisite thirty-six states ratified the amendment and it became a part of the Constitution on February 25, 1913. The federal government now had a source of revenue that would enable it to expand its role in the American economy and society. A rare cartoon that viewed the income tax in a positive light appeared after Congress had enacted a new income tax law in 1913. In the *Des Moines Register and Leader,* Darling depicts Uncle Sam as a barber who is about to trim the locks of a "Little Rich Boy" while close-cropped but smiling urchins look on approvingly through the window. Though the attitude toward the income tax reflected in this cartoon is partially the result of the change in public opinion from 1894 to 1913, it is also important to remember that Des Moines is far removed from New York City, the financial nerve center of the industrial northeast and the home of *Judge* and *Puck,* the two weeklies that published cartoons hostile to the income tax during the 1890s. 🛡

Nineteenth-Century Appointments

CHAPTER 7

Nineteenth-Century Appointments

Supreme Court justices are nominated by the president and confirmed by the Senate. Since George Washington nominated the first six justices on September 26, 1789, presidents have sent nominations to the Senate on one hundred and forty-five occasions. Of these nominations, twenty-eight were unsuccessful either because the Senate rejected or postponed them or because the president withdrew the nominee from consideration. How these failed nominees reacted to their fate varied considerably. The first nominee to be rejected, Justice John Rutledge of South Carolina, nominated by Washington to fill the vacant chief justice chair on July 1, 1795, took his defeat hard. He attempted suicide and later became a mentally disturbed recluse. In contrast, the third rejected nominee, John J. Crittendon of Kentucky, blamed his defeat on the lame-duck status of President John Quincy Adams.

In general, politically weak presidents have had more trouble getting their Supreme Court nominees confirmed than politically strong presidents. In the nineteenth century, vice presidents who entered the nation's highest office by the force of circumstances, rather than by the ballot, had an especially difficult time. John Tyler, who became president on the death of William H. Harrison in 1841, had a reputation of political timidity and five of his six nominees to the Court went down in defeat. Years later, after the Civil War and Abraham Lincoln's assassination, the Senate refused to confirm Andrew Johnson's one and only nominee. Instead, the Republican Congress reduced the number of justices on the Court,

MAKING UP HIS MIND.

SENATOR CONKLING—"Well, I'm good for six years in the Senate, and I've got an offer of the Chief Justice's Chair; but shall I not wait for the White House?"

more or less insuring that Lincoln's Democratic successor would not get a chance to appoint a justice to the Supreme Court.

During the nineteenth century, it took some presidents many months to fill a vacancy on the high court. For instance, when Chief Justice Salmon Chase died on May 8, 1873, President Ulysses S. Grant offered the Court's center seat to seven people over a nine-month period. Four of these individuals declined to be considered for the job, including Roscoe Conkling, the New York senator whose presidential ambitions were well known. On October 4, 1873, Joseph Keppler drew a cartoon for *Frank Leslie's Illustrated Newspaper* that humorously sums up the situation. Grant is tempting Conkling with the judicial robes of a lifetime appointment, but Conkling asks, "shall I not wait for the White House?" Grant's pursuit of Conkling was not the first time a president has tried to eliminate a rival by placing him on the Supreme Court. Historians generally agree that Andrew Jackson's appointment of John McLean in 1829 and Abraham Lincoln's of Salmon Chase in 1864 were both at least partly motivated by such a concern.

On January 31, 1874, a cartoon appeared in *Frank Leslie's Illustrated* that compared Grant's attempt to fill the chair of chief justice to "The Great National Circus." The focal point of the cartoon is a "hoop" of Senate confirmation that a Grant nominee must first jump through before he can sit in the prized chair. Two of the aspirants have already failed to make the leap. George Williams, a former senator from Oregon and Grant's attorney general, is declared by "Ringmaster Grant" to have been "too small a man," a reference to William's undistinguished record and his reputation as a frontier lawyer ill-prepared to decide complex commercial cases. In contrast, Grant describes Caleb Cushing, a former diplomat and

No. 957—Vol. XXXVII.] NEW YORK, JANUARY 31, 1874. [Price, 10 Cents.

THE GREAT NATIONAL CIRCUS.

ACCOMPANIED BY MATT CARPENTER'S UNRIVALED BRASS AND WIND BAND, NOW EXHIBITING TO IMMENSE CROWDS, AND SHOWING THE FAMOUS GROUND AND LOFTY TUMBLINGS FOR THE CHIEF-JUSTICE'S CHAIR.

RING-MASTER GRANT.—"Williams couldn't hit the hoop, and Cushing is too heavily weighted. Now, Roscoe, make a big jump, and you'll go through, and into the seat. Hoop la!"

WAITING.

attorney general under President Franklin Pierce, as "too heavily weighted," probably an allusion to Cushing's shifts in party allegiance. Cushing had started out as a Whig, but became a Democrat in 1841 and a Republican in 1861.

The cartoon portrays Grant as dismissing Conkling's chances (he will "surely tumble short") in favor of Morrison Waite—"a light 'Waite' who . . . can go through the hoop." Though respected and well liked in his home state of Ohio, Waite did not gain national prominence until he was appointed one of the counsels to represent the United States at the Geneva Arbitration Tribunal in 1871. The purpose of this tribunal was to arbitrate the so-called *Alabama* claims. During the Civil War, Confederate cruisers built in British shipyards (the *Florida* and *Alabama*) had sunk thousands of tons of northern shipping. The United States sought compensation from Britain and the two countries agreed to arbitrate the dispute. In 1872, the tribunal awarded the United States $15.5 million, which turned Waite and his two co-counsel into instant celebrities. Grant nominated Waite on January 19, 1874, and he was quickly confirmed two days later, thereby ending the nine-month "circus." Of course, the cartoon's identification of Waite as a "light 'Waite'" is a clear suggestion that he, never having held judicial office or argued a case before the Supreme Court, lacked the qualifications to be chief justice.

The perception that a nominee is too close to the president who appointed him has at times stopped or slowed a confirmation. Stanley Matthews, for example, was a classmate of Rutherford B. Hayes at Kenyon College in the late 1830s. During the Civil War, he served under Hayes in the Twenty-third Ohio Volunteer Infantry. In the disputed election of 1876, which pitted Hayes against Samuel Tilden, the Democratic nominee, Matthews argued on Hayes's behalf before the Electoral Commission. The commission, composed of eight Republicans and seven Democrats, awarded all contested electoral votes to Hayes—by a vote of 8 to 7. Democrats howled that the election had been stolen by the Republicans, but Hayes became president. On January 26, 1881, Hayes picked Matthews to fill the seat on the Court vacated by Noah H. Swayne, but the nomination stalled in the Senate, largely because of Matthews's association with railroad interests. To the surprise of many, incoming President James A. Garfield re-nominated Matthews immediately on entering office in March. On April 20, 1881, *Puck* ran a cartoon by James Albert Walles depicting the tense situation. Matthews is sitting on the "anxious seat" as Garfield searches for the right key to unlock the "deadlocked" Senate. In the end, after two months of heated debate, the Senate confirmed Matthews by a vote of 24 to 23, making him the third justice to be confirmed after his first nomination had failed.

On February 24, 1882, eight years after Roscoe Conkling had turned down Grant's offer to nominate him chief justice, Republican President Chester Arthur, who took office in 1881 after Garfield's assassination, renewed the effort to entice the powerful senator from New York onto the Supreme Court. The nomination was not a complete surprise, if only because Conkling had at one time been Arthur's political mentor in New York's Republican Party. After considering his options for several days, Conkling accepted the nomination. Adhering to its tradition of not rejecting colleagues, the Senate confirmed Conkling's nomination by a vote of 39 to 12 on March 2. Five days later, however, after he had thanked his fellow senators for their support, Conkling reversed course and declined the appointment, thereby becoming the seventh and last person to decline an appoint-

ARTHUR'S AWKWARD "WHITE ELEPHANT.'
"How shall I ever get rid of him? It won't do for me to have him on my hands in 1884!"

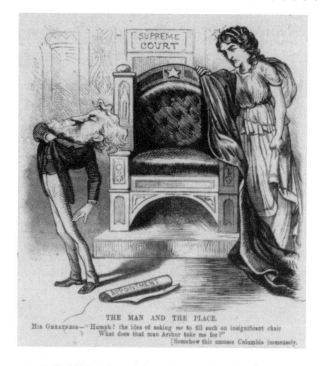

THE MAN AND THE PLACE.

His Greatness.—"Humph! the idea of asking *me* to fill such an insignificant chair
What does that man Arthur take me for?"

[Somehow this amuses Columbia immensely.

DECLINED WITH THANKS.

CONKLING.—"NO, THANK YOU, I DON'T CARE TO BE SHELVED."

ment to the Court (or elevation to chief justice) after having been confirmed by the Senate.

Cartoonists enthusiastically took up the subject of Conkling's decision to decline a Supreme Court appointment. One was published in *Puck*, a magazine allied with the Democratic Party. It portrays Conkling as Arthur's "Awkward White Elephant" who he wants to "get rid of" because it "won't do" to have him "on hand" in 1884, the year of the next presidential election. If the cartoon's insinuation is correct, it would seem that Conkling was twice offered a seat on the Court by two sitting presidents because they both feared him as a possible rival—a testament to Conkling's reputation as a shrewd and formidable politician. On the other hand, the cartoon does not express any regret about Conkling's refusal to join the Court. In the background, a happy Uncle Sam holds a paper reporting Conkling's decision. Behind him, on the wall of the Supreme Court, appear the words "For this relief much thanks," and signed "U.S." Perhaps Conkling was a masterful politician, but that did not mean that he was a suitable choice for a seat on America's high court.

Two cartoons published on March 18 took opposite points of view of what could be called Conkling's snub of the Court. The one that appeared in *Frank Leslie's Illustrated*, entitled "The Man and the Place," refers to Conkling as "His Greatness" and depicts him as a "small man" with a big head who rejects the appointment to such an "insignificant chair." Columbia, her arm resting on a large Supreme Court chair, is amused at Conkling's pomposity. In contrast, *Judge*, a magazine with Republican sympathies, published a cartoon drawn by Walles that flattered Conkling for his good sense in declining the appointment. Arthur is shown at the window of the White House ready to spring a trap baited with a "Supreme Bench." A nattily-dressed Conkling declines to step into the trap commenting, "I don't care to be shelved." The thrust of the cartoon is that the Supreme Court appointment was Arthur's attempt to "trap" Conkling in an "obscure place" on the Supreme Court. *The New York Times* speculated that Conkling refused the appointment because the salary of a Supreme Court justice was not large enough. In any event, Conkling returned to New York City where he made a fortune in the private practice of law.

During the 1890s, a conflict arose between President Grover Cleveland and New York Senator David Hill concerning "senatorial courtesy" and appointments to the Supreme Court. "Senatorial courtesy" is the long-standing tradition by which a nominee to any federal judgeship will not be confirmed by the Senate if the senator of the state in which the appointment will be made is a member of the President's party and opposes the nomination. Though Cleveland and Hill were both New York Democrats, they had been rivals for years. Moreover, though Cleveland won the presidency in 1892, Hill's faction largely controlled New York. When Justice Samuel Blatchford, who was from New York, died in 1893, Cleveland was determined to replace him with someone from the same state. Hill recommended a number of individuals for this "New York" seat on the Supreme Court, but Cleveland ignored him and nominated William B. Hornblower, a staunch member of Cleveland's faction in the New York Democratic Party.

Unfortunately for Hornblower, the year before he had conducted an investigation into the election of a judge to the New York Court of Appeals. The contested election resulted in the defeat of Isaac H. Maynard, a friend and ally of Senator Hill, who retaliated against Hornblower in 1893 by invoking senatorial courtesy to defeat his nomination to the Supreme Court. A cartoon that appeared in the *St.*

Will He Go Over the Bridge or Down the Bank.
"FALSELY, FALSELY MURDERED!"

GROVER: Peck Him, Wheeler! Peck Him!

Louis Post-Dispatch on January 14, 1894, predicts the outcome. It shows Hill strangling a startled Hornblower under the caption, "Falsely, Falsely Murdered!" The very next day the Senate rejected Hornblower by a vote of 30 to 24. The tradition of senatorial courtesy had proven stronger than either Hornblower's qualifications or Cleveland's support.

Not to be intimidated, Cleveland immediately nominated Wheeler H. Peckham, a New York Democrat who had earlier sided with Cleveland against Hill in a patronage dispute. Hill once again invoked senatorial courtesy. A cartoon published in the *New York World* on January 23, 1894, uses the names of Grover's two nominees to place the political situation in comic relief. Grover Cleveland holds a fighting cock in front of Hill's face, shouting, "Peck him, Wheeler! Peck him!" Hornblower is depicted as a crushed horn lying under Hill's left foot. Despite Wheeler's "peckish" defense of his record, the tradition of senatorial courtesy withstood Cleveland's challenge. On February 16, by a margin of 41 to 32, the Senate rejected Peckham's nomination to the Court. W. A. Rogers drew a cartoon entitled "Senatorial Courtesies—Triumph" that artfully expressed his contempt for what Hill had done. With an impish grin on his face and an evil glint in his eye, Hill sits on the hilt of a knife that is stabbing through the nominations of both Hornblower and Peckham. Appearing on the blade of the knife is the ominous word "Malice," a sentiment far removed from any sort of "courtesy."

Frustrated, Cleveland announced that he had run out of "appropriate" New York nominees and nominated Louisiana Senator Edward Douglas White, the Democratic Majority Leader of the Senate. Hill could not invoke senatorial courtesy against his colleague and White was unanimously confirmed on the same day that the Senate received his nomination: February 19, 1894. Accordingly, though Hill won two nomination battles by invoking senatorial courtesy, it is arguable that he lost the war. Cleveland outmaneuvered him by giving the traditional New York seat on the Supreme Court to a popular senator from another state. In 1895, after Justice Howell E. Jackson of Tennessee died, Cleveland again looked to his home state of New York. He first re-nominated Hornblower, but the latter wisely declined the nomination. Then, hoping to avoid another impasse, Cleveland wrote a letter to Hill asking him to support the nomination of Rufus W. Peckham, the brother of Wheeler H. Peckham, whom Hill had opposed the year before. Perhaps realizing that invoking senatorial courtesy would encourage Cleveland to nominate someone from a different state, Hill set aside his "malice" and did not oppose Peckham's nomination. Cleveland was finally able to get one of his New York nominees to the Supreme Court past Hill and over the barrier of senatorial courtesy. 📖

SENATORIAL COURTESIES—TRIUMPH.

The Nineteenth Amendment

CHAPTER 8

The Nineteenth Amendment

Woman Suffrage

The Nineteenth Amendment, which granted women the right to vote in national and state elections, was ratified in 1920, seventy-two years after a resolution calling for woman suffrage was introduced at a convention held in Seneca Falls, New York, in 1848. This resolution was one of several included in the Declaration of Sentiments, a document that addressed a wide range of political, economic, social, and religious issues involving gender equality. All the resolutions contained in the declaration passed unanimously except the one dealing with suffrage, which gained only the support of a narrow majority of the three hundred people (including forty men) in attendance. Those who voted against the suffrage resolution feared that it would give the women's movement an overly radical image. In partial confirmation of this fear, both the press and the pulpit ridiculed and denounced the declaration immediately upon its publication. Reacting to the public outcry, many of the men and women who had signed the declaration withdrew their names. Obviously, in 1848, it was far from obvious that women would ever have the right to vote.

Under the leadership of Elizabeth Cady Stanton, Susan B. Anthony, and Lucy Stone, suffragists engaged in a variety of activities to promote woman suffrage during the 1850s. They raised money, published and distributed books and pamphlets, organized conventions, ran lecture tours, attended legislative hearings, and carried out petition drives. Though these kinds of political activities were suspended during the Civil War, women quickly resurrected

THE MODERN CORNELIA—A VERITABLE RUM 'UN.

"These are my jewels!"

their demand for the franchise at the war's end. The politics of Reconstruction, however, posed the question of who should get the vote first: the newly freed slaves or women? The option of universal suffrage, granting the right to vote to both groups, was perceived by many to be too extreme. A cartoon published on July 31, 1869, in *Frank Leslie's Illustrated Newspaper* parodied this alternative as a "veritable rum 'un." Universal suffrage is depicted as "The Modern Cornelia," an allusion to the aristocratic Roman mother of the second century B.C. who, after her husband's death, dedicated her life to educating her two sons. When asked why she didn't wear any jewelry, the classical Cornelia purportedly pointed to her two sons, who later became important reformers of the Roman state, and remarked that they were her jewels. In the cartoon, the modern Cornelia says the same thing in reference to her children, but the sarcasm is obvious. Not only is she pictured as a tramp, but her two children (Negro and Female Suffrage) are represented, respectively, as a shiftless, dangerous-looking black man and a dowdy old maid cradling a "Sorosis" club. Sorosis was the name of a women's club that had formed in New York after women journalists were barred from a lecture given by Charles Dickens to the New York Press Club in 1868.

After the Republican Party proposed the Fifteenth Amendment, which gave the newly freed slaves the right to vote, women in the suffrage movement could either support it as a step in the direction of universal suffrage or oppose it on the ground that it left the states free to exclude women from the franchise. In 1869, the movement split over this difficult choice. Stanton and Anthony opposed the Fifteenth Amendment and formed the National Woman Suffrage Association (NWSA), while Lucy Stone supported it and organized the American Woman Suffrage Association (AWSA). The Fifteenth Amendment was ratified in 1870.

In 1871, Anthony and Stanton associated NWSA with Victoria Woodhull, a former prostitute and spiritualist who advocated "free love." Though Woodhull's contact with the organization only lasted a year, membership in NWSA plummeted under a deluge of public criticism. A Thomas Nast cartoon published in 1872 indirectly reveals the depth of the public's animosity for Woodhull. She is pictured as Mrs. Satan unsuccessfully tempting a wife to follow her with a banner advocating free love. The dutiful wife, burdened with children and a drunken husband, expresses her resolve to stay on her hard and rocky path of matrimony. The following year, Woodhull accused Henry Ward Beecher, president of the AWSA, of having an affair with Elizabeth Tilton, the wife of a former head of NWSA. Though a jury acquitted Beecher of any wrongdoing, the political damage to the suffrage movement was substantial.

Perhaps because the political situation made it unlikely that Congress would approve a new Sixteenth Amendment, NWSA changed tactics in the early 1870s. Anthony and Stanton began to argue that the already ratified Fourteenth Amendment made women citizens of the United States and, as citizens, states could not exclude them from the franchise. Relying on this argument, Anthony was able to cast a ballot in the presidential election of 1872 in New York, though she was convicted of illegal voting. Stanton wanted to take her case to the Supreme Court, but the trial judge thwarted her plan by refusing to order her to pay the one-hundred-dollar fine. The issue of the relationship of the Fourteenth Amendment to women's rights nonetheless came before the Supreme Court in two pivotal cases during the 1870s. In *Bradwell v. Illinois* (1874), the Court ruled that the Privileges and Immunities Clause of the Fourteenth Amendment did not give women a federal right to practice

"GET THEE BEHIND ME, (MRS.) SATAN"
Wife (with heavy burden). *"I'd rather travel the hardest path of matrimony than follow your footsteps."*

REAL vs. IMAGINARY WANTS.

Misses Anthony and Dickinson and Mrs. Stanton— "We hold that this gives women the right to vote. Any way, you might let us."
Chief Justice Waite— "In the opinion of the Court the XIV. Amendment does not confer on women the right of suffrage."
Public Opinion— "And you might add, Mr. Chief Justice, that the great question of the day is: How to improve the suffrage—not how to extend it."

FEMALE SUFFRAGE.
Wouldn't it put just a little too much power into the hands
of Brigham Young, and his tribe?

law, which meant that states could bar women from the legal profession. In *Minor v. Happersett* (1875), the Court unanimously ruled that the Fourteenth Amendment did not give women the right to vote. A cartoon by Weldon entitled "Real v. Imaginary Wants" commented on this case in the October 21 issue of the *Daily Graphic*. Anthony, Stanton, and Anna Dickinson present their argument that the Fourteenth Amendment gives women the right to vote; Chief Justice Waite and his colleagues deny their claims; and public opinion endorses the result. A feminine Columbia looks with dismay and disdain at the suffragists, who are dressed in men's clothing and have a masculine air.

While NWSA pursued its strategy at the national level, Lucy Stone and AWSA worked to obtain the right to vote in western states and territories. Their more local and incremental

approach was viable because the federal Constitution did not bar states from granting women the right to vote. States and territories were free to give women the right to vote in both local and federal elections. AWSA's strategy was also valuable because it was likely that no federal amendment granting women the right to vote would be ratified until a substantial number of states enfranchised women. In 1869, the territory of Wyoming took the first step by granting women the franchise. A cartoon published in that same year hinted that the Mormon Church would get far too much power if the federal government would permit the territory of Utah to follow Wyoming's example. The Utah territory nonetheless gave women the right to vote in 1870.

Wyoming was accepted into the Union with woman suffrage in 1890, the year NWSA and AWSA united into the National American Woman Suffrage Association (NAWSA) under the combined leadership of Stanton, Anthony, and Stone. Colorado made the move in 1893, followed by Idaho in 1896, the same year Utah became a state. From 1896 until 1910, the woman suffrage movement made no progress, but then the logjam began to break, perhaps in part because of the rising Progressive Movement and the belief that women, if granted the right to vote, would support the Progressive goals of ending child labor, improving health and safety, and enacting pure food and drug legislation. In any case, one after the other, Washington (1910), California (1911), Oregon (1912), Kansas (1912), and Arizona (1912) granted women the right to vote.

A cartoon published by Herbert Perry in the *Sioux City* (Iowa) *Journal* expresses the perceived impact that the extension of woman suffrage in the western states would have on the presidential election of 1912. It shows three little boys—Woody, Teddy, and Will, representing Woodrow Wilson, Theodore Roosevelt, and William Howard Taft—crowding around a pot of 1,400,000 women's votes, each trying to get as many "doughnuts" as he can. The cartoon's implication is that, given the number of women voting in the west, presidential candidates could no longer ignore women's concerns or avoid paying a penalty at the polls if they continued to oppose a federal amendment granting women the right to vote.

WOMEN TO CUT SOME FIGURE THIS YEAR.

There's a Reason

A few years after Wilson's election in 1912, Alice Paul, a militant suffragist who picketed the White House and helped organize the National Woman's Party, advocated that women voters should punish Wilson and the Democratic Party because they had failed to enfranchise women at the national level. This policy was too extreme for the more moderate NAWSA. As a cartoon published in 1913 by French in the *Chicago Record Herald* exemplifies, most cartoonists depicted any association of the suffrage movement with radical causes and militant tactics as counterproductive. A well-dressed little girl walks arm in arm with Billy Ballot under an Equal Rights umbrella while little "Militancy," tattered and bedraggled, is left wondering why she can't get a "feller."

Elected President of NAWSA in 1915, Carrie Chipman Catt played a vital role in the final push for the Nineteenth Amendment. After a number of victories at the state level, she unleashed a massive lobbying effort in Congress. In 1918, President Wilson reversed course and supported a federal amendment. Congress quickly followed suit, approving the Nineteenth Amendment and submitting it to the states for ratification in June 1919. At the state level, the suffragists were ultimately successful, but the contests were often quite close. For example, on August 18, 1920, Tennessee, the crucial thirty-sixth state, ratified the amendment by a single vote when Harry Burn, yielding to his elderly mother's wishes, switched sides and voted for the amendment. The irony is that, as a cartoon by

John Francis Knott published in the *Dallas News* reveals quite humorously, both political parties took credit for the amendment in the presidential elections later that year. To the surprise of a young woman in the political garden of Eden, both political parties assert "It was my rib," when in fact the amendment was the result of a seventy-two-year effort by women themselves. ⚖

The two Adams: It was my rib, Eve!

Prohibition

CHAPTER 9

Prohibition

Only once in American history has an amendment to the Constitution been repealed in its entirety. In 1919, the Eighteenth Amendment prohibiting "the manufacture, sale, or transportation of intoxicating liquors" was ratified by a wide margin. Ultimately, only one state—Rhode Island—refused to support it. Fourteen years later, by an equally wide margin, the Twenty-First Amendment was ratified, with South Carolina the only state voting against the repeal of national prohibition. Rarely has this country experienced such a radical turnabout in public opinion. Today most commentators agree that the policy of national prohibition was a failure and the effort to control alcohol use by amending the Constitution a mistake.

Under the prodding of the American Temperance Movement, several states imposed legal restrictions on alcohol during the 1830s and 1840s. In 1846, Maine became the first state to enact a state prohibition law. Following the Civil War, new temperance groups arose: the Prohibition Party in 1869; the Women's Christian Temperance Union in 1873; and, finally, in 1893, the Anti-Saloon League, the organization that would play a crucial role in the passage of the Eighteenth Amendment. Despite these organizational developments, the gains of the prohibitionist forces were modest. By 1900, only five states had adopted statewide prohibition laws. A cartoon that appeared in *Puck* on July 3, 1889, reflects late-nineteenth-century social attitudes toward alcohol. Mr. Prohibition, an old man holding an umbrella, is getting a "cold reception" from women, who were at the time thought

A COLD RECEPTION EVERYWHERE.

OPEN SEASON
A Post-Dispatch Cartoonist Upon the Uprising in the Various Legislatures.

to be the movement's most likely allies. Though this cartoon perhaps exaggerates the degree of hostility to prohibition during the 1880s, it highlights the opposing social attitudes concerning alcohol that existed at the end of the nineteenth century.

In part because of the movement's association with other reform efforts, such as progressivism, the fortunes of prohibition improved markedly in the early years of the twentieth century. State after state imposed new restrictions on alcohol or adopted statewide prohibition. A cartoon published on January 10, 1907, in the *St. Louis Post-Dispatch* echoes these developments. A mob of states are depicted as bomb-throwing Russian revolutionaries who have declared "open season" on Czar Booze and the Grand Dukes Nick-otine and Bacchus. In 1913, as a part of this trend in favor of tighter state controls on alcohol, Congress enacted the Webb-Kenyon Act, which enabled dry states for the first time to prohibit interstate shipments of liquor to consumers. The Supreme Court upheld this law in *Clark Distilling Company v. Western Maryland Railway Company* (1917). By 1916, nineteen states had statewide prohibition and many of the others granted local communities the right to prohibit the manufacture and sale of alcohol. Prohibition sentiment was clearly gaining ground.

In the early years of the twentieth century, the prohibitionists focused their efforts on curbing alcohol use at the state level. The Anti-Saloon League had advocated a constitutional amendment in 1913, but its proposal failed to pass the House of Representatives in 1914. In 1917, however, Congress enacted the Lever Act, which established national prohibition as a wartime measure to save grain for the troops. In December of the same year, again acting under the pressure of the war effort, Congress submitted the Eighteenth Amendment to the states. Ratification was completed by thirty-

Across!

six of the forty-eight states by January 16, 1919. A cartoon drawn by Orr for the *Chicago Tribune* commemorated the event by featuring "Eliza Prohibition" carrying her infant across dangerous waters to the safety of ratification as hound-dog distillers howl in the background. By 1922, all the states save Rhode Island ratified the amendment, even though a popular referendum in Ohio attempted to rescind the earlier state legislature's vote in favor of it. In *Hawke v. Smith* (1920), the Supreme Court upheld Congress's power to decide how states must ratify amendments. Since the Eighteenth Amendment referred to ratification by state legislatures, the Ohio referendum was null and void.

According to the terms of the Eighteenth Amendment, the manufacture, sale, and transportation of intoxicating liquors would become illegal one year after its ratification and both the states and the federal government would have concurrent enforcement powers. Late in 1919, before the amendment took effect, Congress enacted the Volstead Act, which outlawed both beer and wine by defining "intoxicating liquors" as any beverage over 0.5 percent alcohol. Legally speaking, this strict

Somebody Is Kicking His Houn' Around Just Now

THAT NON-REFILLABLE BOTTLE

definition put the country's seventh largest industry (all liquor, wine, and beer manufacturers, distributors, and retailers) out of business. Only the Thirteenth Amendment, which freed approximately four million slaves, had a comparable impact on property rights.

Fighting back in court, opponents of prohibition challenged the constitutionality of the Eighteenth Amendment. First, they argued that the amendment had not been legally submitted to the states by Congress because it had been passed only by a two-thirds majority of those present, not by a two-thirds majority of the total membership of both houses. Second, they insisted that the Eighteenth Amendment was an illegal violation of the Tenth Amendment because it authorized the intrusion of the federal government into a policy area that had traditionally been reserved to the states. In the context of this litigation, the *Baltimore Sun* published a cartoon showing the "prohibition hound" on the loose, causing all sorts of trouble. At the bottom, and off to the side, a little man standing by a sign pointing to the Supreme Court remarks that prohibition "may not last long."

The prediction that the Supreme Court might invalidate the Eighteenth Amendment did not prove accurate. In the *National Prohibition Cases* (1920), the Supreme Court refused to recognize any judicially enforceable limits to the amendment power outlined in the Constitution. Two cartoons that appeared at the time express the finality of the Court's decision. One, published in the *New York Times* on June 13, 1920, shows a "wet" staring at a "non-refillable bottle" that is "corked" by the Supreme Court decision. The other, drawn by McCarthy and published in the *New Orleans Times-Picayune,* features Mr. Prohibition reading from the Court's decision in front of a cobwebbed grave littered with whiskey bottles over the caption

Telling the corpse he's dead

"Telling the corpse he's dead." It was common for cartoonists of this era to symbolize prohibition by drawing the grave of "John Barleycorn," a centuries-old personification of the grain from which malt liquor is made.

In the 1920s, the Supreme Court decided a number of cases involving the Eighteenth Amendment and the Volstead Act. In one of these decisions, *Cunard Steamship Company, et al. v. Mellon* (1923), the Court ruled that the federal government could not enforce prohibition on American ships beyond the three-mile limit. This decision is highlighted in two cartoons of the period. In one, published on May 5, 1923, in the *St. Louis Post-Dispatch*, the Court reins in a camel, a symbol often used to represent the "drys," preventing it from swimming too far from shore. In the other, published a day later in the *New York Times*, the Court is leading a séance that, unless it's a "mirage," is putting "American shipping" in touch with the spirit of John Barleycorn. Reflecting evolving public opinion, both cartoons express a somewhat negative outlook on prohibition.

Though the Court in *Cunard* confined prohibition to the United States and its actual territories, most of its decisions

THE SEANCE—SPIRIT OR MIRAGE?

A PINT OF WHISKY
EVERY TEN DAYS
IS ENOUGH

A DAY IN THE U. S. SUPREME COURT.

during the twenties upheld vigorous enforcement of the Volstead Act and an expansive reading of the Eighteenth Amendment. In *United States v. Lanza* (1922), the Court gave a broad reading of the provision granting both Congress and the states the power to enforce the amendment. It upheld warrantless automobile searches in *Carroll v. United States* (1925) and wiretapping in *Olmstead v. United States* (1928), both of which had become commonplace in the fight to control illegal smuggling and bootlegging. In *Lambert v. Yellowly* (1926), it ruled that, under the Eighteenth Amendment, Congress had the power to limit the amount of liquor a physician could prescribe

for a patient to one pint every ten days. Daniel R. Fitzpatrick lampooned this decision in a cartoon entitled "A Day in the U.S. Supreme Court" that the *St. Louis Post-Dispatch* published on November 30, 1926. It shows a justice peering into law book after law book and then announcing that a pint every ten days is enough. The sarcastic inference was that the Court was making a ruling on a subject about which it knew nothing.

Though the Court upheld enforcement of the Volstead Act, the American public became more and more disenchanted with prohibition during the 1920s. Given the opportunities for huge profits, organized crime and corruption grew rapidly dur-

LIKE FLIES AROUND A SUGAR BARREL

ing prohibition, and the government responded in ways that heightened the fears of civil libertarians. A cartoon published on July 23, 1925, by Rollin Kirby in the *St. Louis Post-Dispatch* focuses on this problem. Officials living off the profits of the illegal manufacture and sale of alcohol are depicted as flies around the "sugar barrel" of the Eighteenth Amendment.

Alcohol consumption did go down during prohibition, but the degree of non-compliance was so large, especially in cities, that it threatened to encourage disrespect for law in general. A cartoon published on August 8, 1928, in the *New York American* hints at the corrosive effect prohibition was having on the law-abiding character of the American people. While hiding the "cigar" of the Fourteenth Amendment behind its back, Congress admonishes the public not to smoke the "cigarette" of the Eighteenth Amendment. The cartoonist's point is that Congress had no right to complain about the public's disobedience of the Eighteenth Amendment until it complied with the Fourteenth by reapportioning Congress. In 1928, urban dwellers, who tended to oppose prohibition, were underrepresented in the House of Representatives because that body had not reapportioned itself since the 1910 census.

Hasn't Missed Yet!

Though public dissatisfaction with prohibition grew throughout the 1920s, repeal of the Eighteenth Amendment seemed a virtual impossibility. It would require a change of mind of at least one-third of Congress and half the states. Despite the odds, the Association Against the Prohibition Amendment (AAPA), the new counterpart to the Anti-Saloon League, insisted that repeal was the only option that would preserve the rule of law, civil liberties, and public integrity. In part because of AAPA's efforts, prohibition became a major issue in the presidential election of 1928, even though, in the end, the Democratic candidate and opponent of prohibition, New York Governor Alfred E. Smith, lost to Herbert Hoover.

Four years later, however, after the onset of the Great Depression, Franklin Delano Roosevelt was elected on a Democratic platform that called for the repeal of the Eighteenth Amendment. Viewing the election as a mandate against prohibition, Congress proposed the Twenty-First Amendment on February 20, 1933. The social-political atmosphere can be gleaned from a cartoon published in the *New York American* on June 23, 1933. It shows a gunner in a "prohibition shooting gallery" picking off fourteen states one by one without a miss. It is possible that the quick success of the repeal movement was largely a result of the fact that Congress, for the first and only time ever, had specified in the Twenty-First Amendment that special state conventions, not state legislatures, were to decide whether to ratify the amendment or not. In any case, by December 5, 1933, in less time than it took to ratify the Eighteenth Amendment, the requisite thirty-six states voted in favor of repealing prohibition and only one state—South Carolina—voted against it. On October 15, 1933, Fitzpatrick in the *St. Louis Post-Dispatch* memorialized the event with a cartoon showing Mr. Prohibition diving into New York Harbor. In the corner of the cartoon is a small reprint of the cartoon of a diving Statute of Liberty that Fitzpatrick had published after the Eighteenth Amendment had been ratified. The juxtaposition of the two cartoons neatly encapsulates the American experience with prohibition. ▨

(FROM THE POST-DISPATCH, JAN. 16, 1919.)

"34—35—36!"

The New Deal

JUST A MINUTE! NOT SO FAST!
SUPREME COUR
CONGRESS
TO THE JUMPING OFF PLACE.

CHAPTER 10

The New Deal

The Great Depression of 1929 produced a constitutional crisis of major proportions. The basic question was whether the federal government had the legal authority to respond to the plight of the millions of people who were hungry, homeless, or unemployed. Placing his faith in the self-correcting powers of an unregulated private economy, Republican President Herbert Hoover refused to do much of anything at the federal level. In November 1932, the American people rejected Hoover's *laissez-faire* approach by electing Democrat Franklin Delano Roosevelt president of the United States. A cartoon by Elizabeth Enright that appeared in the *New York American* on March 23, 1933, just a few weeks after FDR's inauguration as president, humorously depicts the frenzied pace of legislation that resulted from the change of administrations. FDR is raking all the "National Emergency" problems into a hole in his desk, each problem turning into a happy bill that then runs off to Congress. Though many of FDR's initiatives were unprecedented federal attempts to regulate banking, agriculture, finance, labor, and manufacturing, the seventy-third Congress enacted most of them within the first hundred days of the new administration, including the Tennessee Valley Authority (TVA), the National Industry Recovery Act (NIRA), and the Agricultural Adjustment Act (AAA). Enright hints at the emerging constitutional crisis in a cartoon published on June 17. A smiling old man representing Congress throws down his "Emergency Legislation Gun" after he has shot the federal Constitution full of holes.

Action

ENRIGHT

Shot Full of Holes

ENRIGHT

At the time, it was unclear how the Supreme Court would react to FDR's attempt to impose a federal scheme of regulation on the national economy. Would the Court uphold these controversial laws or invalidate them? At first, things looked promising for the New Deal. In *Home Building and Loan Association v. Blaisdell* (1934), the Court upheld a Minnesota law that granted relief to people who could not pay their mortgages. Though behind in their payments, mortgagees received protection from foreclosure if they paid a "reasonable" rental fee to their bank or loan association, a fee that was smaller than their normal mortgage payment. The question was whether such a "mortgage moratorium" law violated Article I, Section 10 of the Constitution, which forbids the states from passing any "Law impairing the Obligation of Contracts." In a narrow 5 to 4 vote, the majority of the justices ruled in favor of the law on the ground that in an emergency a government could do things it could not otherwise do. The event was memorialized in a cartoon that appeared in the *Cleveland Plain Dealer*. A gleeful New Dealer, his hands full of emergency legislation, watches as the Minnesota Mortgage Moratorium law proudly parades down the steps of the Supreme Court. Dell's caption, "WELL, *HE* GOT THROUGH," suggests that the result in *Blaisdell* was somewhat of a surprise and hints that other New Deal laws might not fare as well.

Dell's prediction turned out to be true. In January 1935, the Court decided *Panama Refining Co. v. Ryan,* a case dealing with a provision of the NIRA that gave the president the power to limit interstate shipments of oil for the purpose of maintaining oil prices and conserving resources. The Court ruled that this "hot oil" provision involved an unconstitutional delegation of legislative power to the executive branch because it established no clear standards for the president to exercise his dis-

"WELL, *HE* GOT THROUGH!"

The Restraining Hand

cretion. The case was an important one because other provisions of the NIRA delegated power to draft "codes of fair competition" that would regulate prices of commodities, wages, and hours of labor, not to the president, but to trade and industrial groups. Such groups would draft the codes and submit them to the president for his approval, which transformed them into law. It seemed likely that these provisions would suffer the same fate as the "hot oil" provision had suffered in *Panama Refining Co.* A cartoon published on January 28, 1935, by Nate Hollier in the *New York American* implicitly welcomed the demise of the NIRA. Appearing next to an editorial calling the Congress that had enacted the NIRA "a national disgrace," the cartoon shows the "long arm" of the Supreme Court preventing Congress from running off a cliff. The editorial warns that "Congress came dangerously near to the automatic yes-yes legislative bodies of the one-man governments in Europe" and describes the recent "hot oil" case as "a powerful whack on the

soles of the feet of a sleeping watchman [Congress] by the guardian of our liberties [the Supreme Court]."

Whether the federal government could nullify gold clauses in private and public contracts was the next New Deal controversy that came before the Supreme Court. Clauses of this type were a safeguard against inflation. They gave the bearers of a bond or a certificate the option of being paid in gold or its monetary equivalent at the time the bond or certificate was redeemed. Since these clauses encouraged public hoarding of gold, Congress nullified them on June 5, 1933. A cartoon published by Ino Cassals in the *Brooklyn Eagle* captures the public's anxiety as the gold clause cases were being considered by the Supreme Court in mid-February 1935. It pictures a worried gold dollar waiting for the verdict. New Deal lawyers argued that, despite gold clauses, the federal government could let bond issuers, including the federal government, pay off contracts with gold clauses in inflated paper dollars because Article I, Section 8

THE
DOLLAR

WAITING FOR THE VERDICT.

of the Constitution gave Congress the power "to coin Money" and "regulate the Value thereof." Defenders of gold insisted that a promise to pay in gold had to be honored, especially if it was the federal government that had made the promise.

Fearful of what the Supreme Court would do, FDR drafted a speech that he intended to deliver if the Court ruled that the nullification of gold clauses was unconstitutional. It contained the following language: "To stand idly by and to permit the decision of the Supreme Court to be carried through to its logical, inescapable conclusion would so imperil the economic and political security of this nation that the executive officers of the Government must look beyond the narrow letter of contractual obligations, so that they may sustain the substance of the promise originally made in accord with the actual intention of

the parties." FDR, however, did not have to carry through with his threat to disregard a Supreme Court decision. Though the Court ruled, in its decision of February 18, 1935, that the federal government could not impair its own obligations by nullifying the gold clauses contained in federal bonds, it upheld Congress's power to nullify gold clauses in private contracts and certificates. The victory for federal bondholders, however, was a hollow one because the Court denied them the right to sue the United States, holding that the damages that they had suffered by the government's nullification of the gold clause were only nominal in character. A Herbert Johnson cartoon published in the *Saturday Evening Post* on April 30, 1935, pokes fun at the result. Though the Court says that the New Deal has no right to assault a female "bond buyer" and her two children ("business confidence" and "sanctity of contracts"), they nevertheless have "no redress."

Schecter v. United States, the Court's long-awaited decision on the constitutionality of the NIRA, finally came down on May 27, 1935. The facts could not have been less favorable for FDR and his administration. Rather than a code of competition dealing with a national industry, such as steel or coal, *Schecter* involved the code of the live poultry industry operating in New York City. The defendants, local slaughterhouse operators who purchased chickens from interstate dealers and sold them to local retailers, had been convicted of a number of violations of the poultry code, including selling an "unfit chicken," which explains why the case became known as the "Sick Chicken" case. The nickname was apt because it implicitly asked whether punishing a person for selling a "sick chicken" could possibly be within the federal government's power to regulate interstate commerce. Two cartoons by Daniel R. Fitzpatrick that appeared in the *St. Louis Post-Dispatch* touched upon this theme. The first, published on May 3, prior to the Court's decision, depicts a chicken trying to hatch the NIRA as it roosts at the Supreme Court. On May 27, the Court ruled that the NIRA was unconstitutional on two grounds: it was an improper delegation of legislative power and an illegitimate attempt to regulate intrastate commercial activity based on Congress's power to regulate interstate commerce. Fitzpatrick's second cartoon, published on

REPUDIATION OF GOLD CLAUSE

NEW DEAL

BOND BUYER

BUSINESS CONFIDENCE

SANCTITY OF CONTRACTS

THE COURT

HE HAD NO RIGHT TO DO IT; BUT, SINCE HE'S DONE IT, YOU HAVE NO REDRESS - NEXT CASE!

Herbert Johnson

June 7, sarcastically pictures "Schecter's chickens" as a "new exhibit" in the animal Hall of Fame.

The Supreme Court's ruling in *Schecter* did not persuade FDR and his New Deal supporters in Congress to back down. In a press conference soon after the decision, FDR criticized the case as being "squarely on the side of restoring to the states forty-eight different controls over national economic problems." Registering its disapproval of what the Court had done, Congress began to consider a number of bills that would impose new federal regulations on the economy. A cartoon by Malone published in the *New York American* on June 10, 1935, reflects the temper of the times. A policeman, symbolizing the

Supreme Court, having already given one ticket to Congress for reckless driving, must nevertheless warn him not to stray from Constitution Avenue.

Despite Malone's warning, on July 5, 1945, Congress passed the National Labor Relations Act (the Wagner Act), which gave workers the right to unionize and bargain collectively, and on August 30, the National Bituminous Coal Conservation Act (the Guffey Coal Act), which imposed directly on a national industry the same kinds of regulations that had been rejected by the Court in *Schecter*. While the latter bill was before Congress, FDR wrote a letter expressing his hope that Congress "will not permit doubts as to constitutionality, however reasonable, to block the suggested legislation." Congress should pass the Coal Act and force the Supreme Court to decide whether the federal government had the necessary power under the commerce clause to regulate a basic national industry.

After the summer of 1935, four major pieces of New Deal legislation were awaiting Supreme Court review. The situation is humorously portrayed in a cartoon by Gene Elderman published in the *Washington Post* on October 11, 1935. It shows the New Deal, an old woman, pleading with the Supreme Court not to send "her boys" to prison. Sitting off to the side are four suspicious-looking individuals, all in irons: the "TVA," the "Guffey Coal Act," the "A[gricultural] A[djustment] A[ct]," and the "Wagner Act." The Tennessee Valley Authority was a New Deal government corporation created to develop the Tennessee River Valley. The authority had the power to construct dams and reservoirs for the purpose of power production and flood control, to manufacture fertilizer and explosives for the War Department, and to improve rivers in the valley for the purpose of both navigation and commerce. The question was whether the federal government had the authority to create such a massive development program. In February 1936, the Court upheld the TVA's constitutionality in *Ashwander v. Tennessee Valley Authority*. One of the New Deal's "boys" was in the clear.

The Agricultural Adjustment Act and the Guffey Coal Act met the opposite fate. The AAA was a New Deal attempt to maintain prices of certain agricultural commodities: wheat, corn, milk, tobacco, rice, and cotton. The law allowed farmers to agree to reduce the number of acres they farmed in exchange for a cash payment that was financed by an excise tax on processors of the relevant commodity. The payment and the tax were calculated to give the commodity the same value it had in the

ROOSTING IN THE SUPREME COURT.

NEW EXHIBIT IN THE HALL OF FAME.

Traffic Warning

1909–1914 period. In January 1936, on the ground that the entire program was an attempt by the federal government to regulate agricultural production, the Court declared the AAA unconstitutional in *United States v. Butler*, a 6 to 3 decision. The gist of the Court's reasoning was that Congress could not use its spending and taxing powers for the purpose of regulating economic activity that it could not regulate under the interstate commerce power. The Guffey Coal Act "imposed" an NIRA-like "code of competition" on the coal industry by imposing a fifteen-percent tax on all coal producers, but remitting it to those producers who complied with the "code." Four months after *Butler*, in another 6 to 3 decision, the Court inval-idated the law in *Carter v. Carter Coal Company*, concluding that the tax was nothing more than a penalty for non-compliance with a code that the federal government had no authority to enact under the commerce power.

Though liberals attacked the Court and its constitutional stand against the New Deal and conservatives sprang to the Court's defense, it was not clear where the majority of the American people stood on the basic issue dividing the country. Did the federal government have the authority to regulate the economy and address the needs of the poor and unemployed, or did these functions belong essentially to the states? The presidential election of 1936 took shape as a popular referendum on this question.

"DON'T SEND MY BOYS TO PRISON!"

CHAPTER 11

FDR's Court-Packing Plan

With forty-six of forty-eight states backing the Democratic Party, the November 1937 election was a landslide victory for FDR and his New Deal policies. Armed with this electoral mandate, FDR went on the offensive in his struggle with the Supreme Court over the constitutionality of his New Deal program. On January 6, 1937, in his annual message to Congress, he insisted that the Constitution was not to blame for the predicament in which the country found itself. "During the past year," he said, "there has been a growing belief that there is little fault to be found with the Constitution of the United States as it stands today. The vital need is not an alteration of our fundamental law, but an increasingly enlightened view with reference to it. Difficulties have grown out of its interpretation; but rightly considered, it can be used as an instrument of progress, and not as a device for prevention of action." He concluded, somewhat ominously, "Means must be found to adapt our legal forms and our judicial interpretation to the actual present national needs." A cartoon drawn by Milton Carlisle for the *Binghamton* (N.Y.) *Press* drew out the implications of FDR's words. It pictures FDR and his ornery "new deal objectives" taking cover from the rain under the Supreme Court's cloak—a symbol of a liberal interpretation of the Constitution. "Isn't this lots better than getting amendments to cover them?" FDR asks. The cartoon is hinting that FDR will not try to increase the federal government's powers by pursuing the slow and cumber-

To Six of the Nine

MESSAGE ON FEDERAL COURT REFORM

RETIRE OR MOVE OVER!

U.S. SUPREME COURT

A FREE AND INDEPENDENT JUDICIARY

the existence of a Supreme Court, it does not say anything about the number of justices. It has therefore been left to Congress to determine the size of the Supreme Court. It fixed the number of justices at six in 1789, five in 1801, six again in 1802, nine in 1837, ten in 1863, seven in 1866, and nine once again in 1869, where it remained until FDR presented his court reform bill to the Democratically-controlled Congress of 1937. Accordingly, if FDR could only get Congress to enact his bill, all his constitutional problems would be over. Six new justices handpicked by FDR would give him the votes on the Court that he needed for a more liberal interpretation of the federal government's power to regulate the economy.

Though the primary purpose of FDR's court reform bill was to "pack" the Supreme Court with New Deal justices, FDR justified the reform on the basis of efficiency, in particular on

some amendment process. Instead he will attempt to convince the Supreme Court to adopt a more expansive understanding of the existing powers of the federal government, in particular Congress's power to regulate interstate commerce.

How FDR planned to induce the Supreme Court to become more flexible in its interpretation of the Constitution did not remain a mystery for long. On February 5, FDR presented Congress with a bill to reorganize the federal judiciary. One of the provisions of the bill provided that the president could appoint an additional judge for those who, having served ten years, refused to resign within six months after their seventieth birthday. Since the bill also fixed the maximum size of the Supreme Court at fifteen, FDR would be able to appoint six new justices to the Supreme Court if it was enacted into law. A cartoon by Lute Pease published in the *Newark* (N.J.) *News* puts the proposal into sharp relief. Entitled "To Six of the Nine," it depicts FDR commanding an old Supreme Court Justice, "Retire or Move Over!" The juxtaposition of FDR's harsh words with the ideal of "A Free and Independent Judiciary" is laden with irony.

One reason why FDR opted for his "retire-or-move-over" approach was quite simple. Though the Constitution mandates

NOT VERY CONVINCING

DON'T THINK IT'S JUST BECAUSE OF HIS DECISIONS I WANT TO CHANGE THE UMPIRE — OH, MY, NO! — IT'S JUST THAT THE POOR OLD MAN LOOKS LIKE HE NEEDS A REST AND SHOULD BE RETIRED AT ONCE, WHILE I'M AT BAT

SUPREME COURT

NEW DEAL

FDR

CONGRESS

THE LATEST WHITE HOUSE "RABBIT" MAKES THE SPOTLIGHT

the ground that old judges were too frail for all the work they had to do. On February 19, 1937, a cartoon drawn by Vaughn Shoemaker that appeared in the *Chicago News* mocks FDR's "efficiency" justification of his court reform package. It compares FDR's bill to a baseball batter's request to switch umpires while he's at the plate, not because of the umpire's decisions, but because the "poor old man looks like he needs a rest." The caption——"Not Very Convincing"——sums up Shoemaker's point.

A significant segment of both Congress and the American public reacted negatively to FDR's ill-disguised court-packing plan. A cartoon published by Henry Brown in the *New York Herald Tribune* reflected the growing opposition. Once the court reform bill——"the latest White House 'Rabbit'" that FDR has pulled out of his hat——enters the spotlight of publicity, everyone can see that it is the skunk of "Supreme Court Control." A terrified spectator, signifying the American public, runs for the exit, while members of the Senate hold their noses and warn each other of the danger. The cartoon aptly captures much of the public's and Congress's indignation at FDR's clever attempt to justify packing the court on grounds of efficiency. Many Democratic members of the Senate, led by Senator Burton K. Wheeler of Montana, withdrew their support for the bill, a fact humorously depicted in a cartoon published by George Evans in the *Columbus* (Ohio) *Dispatch*. A jockey, representing the "Proposal to Pack the Supreme Court," tries to kick the Democratic donkey into motion in the Congressional Ring. Though the donkey's front feet, which symbolize the New Dealers, are ready to move, the hind legs, which symbolize the Constitutional Democrats who oppose FDR's court-packing plan, refuse to budge. They are on a sit-down strike, while a disappointed FDR, whip in his hand, looks on miserably.

---SPEAKING OF SIT-DOWNS

This Three Horse Team Is Pulling Together—By Hungerford

A Palpable Hit

During early 1937, FDR described the American form of government as "a three-horse team provided by the Constitution to the American people so that their field might be plowed." The Congress and the executive, in FDR's opinion, were pulling the plough together, but the courts were not. This metaphor of three horses brought on a deluge of political cartoons picturing FDR as a quasi-dictator directing all three horses of the American government. On March 9, 1937, in one of his trademark fireside chats, FDR responded to this criticism by claiming that it overlooks "the simple fact that the president, as chief executive, is himself one of the three horses. It is the American people themselves who are in the driver's seat. It is the American people themselves who want the fur-

row plowed. It is the American people themselves who expect the third horse to pull in unison with the other two." FDR's attempt at clarification brought on another storm of political "horse" cartoons. One of these, by Cyrus C. Hungerford, published in the *Pittsburgh Post-Gazette* on March 13, 1937, artfully turns FDR's metaphor upside down. It suggests that if FDR gets his court reform proposal enacted, he wouldn't be just one of the horses. He'd be all three horses of the American government and he would trample the "Constitution Fence" to take a "Short Cut to New Deal Pasture."

A few weeks after FDR's fireside chat, Wheeler testified in opposition to the court-reform bill before the Senate Judiciary Committee. During his testimony, he read a letter from Chief Justice Charles Evans Hughes stating that the Supreme Court was "fully abreast of its work" and that there was no "congestion of cases" on the Court's calendar. A cartoon by Charles Henry Sykes published in the *Rochester* (N.Y.) *Democrat and Chronicle* on March 25, 1937, describes Wheeler's tactical use of Hughes's letter as "a palpable hit." Wheeler is pictured plunging the sword of Hughes's letter into the midriff of Roosevelt's court reform plan. FDR's "efficiency" justification for his proposal is pictured in the cartoon as a useless, broken wooden sword.

The more FDR's bill was perceived to be simply a court-packing plan, the more public and congressional support for it shrank. Supreme Court decisions during 1937 contributed to the demise of FDR's plan. From March to June of that year, the Supreme Court upheld four central pieces of New Deal legislation, including the pivotal National Labor Relations Act (NLRA) of 1935 (also known as the Wagner Act) in *National Labor Relations Board v. Jones & Laughlin Steel Corporation*; and the Social Security Act of 1935 in *Steward Machine Company v. Davis*. The NLRA granted workers the right to organize unions in businesses engaged in interstate commerce and prohibited employers from discriminating against employees who joined unions or participated in union activities, while the Social Security Act provided unemployment compensation and old age benefits to employees financed by taxes on employers. At the time, cartoonists of every political stripe commented on the significance

A LITTLE STUDY DOES WONDERS

of these decisions. Evans drew one such cartoon for the *Columbus* (Ohio) *Dispatch* that appeared on March 31, 1937. It portrays the Supreme Court as a teacher who flunked Congress in 1936, but who passed him in 1937, after he had done his homework in constitutional law. "Aunt SAMantha" advises the parent of the boy—FDR—that he had been wrong the year before to blame the boy's poor grades on his teachers. More teachers aren't what the boy needs, but rather "the proper preparation of his work." The cartoon's implication is that FDR had not pressured the Supreme Court into changing course in 1937. Instead, compared to what they had enacted in previous years, Congress and FDR were simply doing a better job of crafting laws that were within the constitutional powers of the federal government.

Kendall Vintroux had a diametrically opposed slant on the Supreme Court's 1937 New Deal decisions. In his cartoon that appeared in the *Charleston* (W.Va.) *Gazette* on April 15, FDR and the Supreme Court reverse the roles they had in Evans's cartoon. The Court is portrayed as a teacher's pet who is trying to win the good graces of FDR by bringing him "apples": *West Coast Hotel v. Parrish,* which sustained a state minimum-wage law for women; and *Jones & Laughlin Steel Corporation,* which, as noted above, upheld the Wagner Act. FDR, not the Supreme Court, is the teacher, and the Constitution is prominently displayed behind him. The general impression left by Vitroux's cartoon is that it is the Supreme Court that had finally learned its lesson, not Congress or the president. The 1937 decisions supporting the constitutionality of New Deal legislation did not indicate "proper preparation" on the part of Congress, as Evans suggests, but rather that the Supreme Court has wisely adopted a more flexible understanding of the Constitution.

In any case, whether it was the threat of an enlarged Court that convinced the justices not to stand in FDR's way or whether it was some other factor that explains why the Court became more tolerant of New Deal legislation, the Court's 1937 decisions doomed FDR's court-reform bill. On June 14, 1937, the Senate Judiciary Committee, by a vote of 10 to 8, reported the bill out unfavorably, and the Senate rejected the bill 70 to 20 on July 22. FDR therefore lost his "court-packing" battle with the Supreme Court, but he may very well have won the war. In 1937, the Supreme Court no longer stood in the way of FDR's New Deal.

Another Apple For The Teacher

Desegregation of
Public Schools

CHAPTER 12

Desegregation of Public Schools

On May 17, 1954, the Supreme Court declared racial segregation in public schools unconstitutional in *Brown v. Board of Education.* "Separate educational facilities are inherently unequal," Chief Justice Earl Warren wrote for a unanimous Court. They generate among African-American children "a feeling of inferiority as to their status in the community that may affect their hearts and minds in a way unlikely ever to be undone." A state could therefore no longer require or authorize racially segregated public schools. The decision, though in principle limited to segregation in public education, cast doubt on the validity of other kinds of "separate-but-equal" public accommodations that were prevalent in the South: for example, separate public beaches, golf courses, toilets, and water fountains. Whether these types of segregated facilities produced "feelings of inferiority" or not, they now arguably failed to satisfy the demands of the Equal Protection Clause of the Fourteenth Amendment. *Brown* therefore marked the beginning of the end of the Jim Crow system of segregation that had permeated the southern way of life for decades.

Popular reaction to the Court's decision in *Brown* varied across the country. To commemorate the occasion, many cartoonists in the North invoked the image of the Liberty Bell. An example is a cartoon drawn by Daniel R. Fitzpatrick that appeared in the *St. Louis Post-Dispatch* on May 18, 1954. The tone of these "Liberty Bell" cartoons resembled that of Warren's opinion in *Brown.* Not

LIBERTY BELL, 1954

wanting to anger southerners, and perhaps thereby encourage resistance to the Court's decision, Warren took a conciliatory approach. In his own words, he wanted the opinion to be "short, readable by the lay public, non-rhetorical, unemotional, and, above all, non-accusatory." He therefore justified the Court's ruling in *Brown* on the ground that evolving social science had discovered that segregation had pernicious effects on black school children. The "Liberty Bell" cartoons are "non-accusatory" in a similar way. They celebrate the end of segregation in public schools without blaming anyone. In contrast, a cartoon by Bruce Shank that appeared on May 19, 1954, in the *Buffalo* (N.Y.) *Evening News* pictures the South as a southern aristocrat watching the smoke of school segregation laws billowing out of his burning mansion. The caption "Gone With the Wind" refers to Margaret Mitchell's popular book by the same title. A fair interpretation of the meaning of Shank's cartoon is that, just as the Civil War destroyed the southern aristocratic life by putting an end to slavery, a theme of Mitchell's novel, so also the Supreme Court's *Brown* decision would destroy the South's racially oppressive Jim Crow society by putting an end to unequal segregated public education.

Cartoonists working for southern newspapers, not surprisingly, had more sympathy for their region's situation. A cartoon by Herc Ficklen published in the *Dallas Morning News* depicts the Supreme Court inviting a southern man to "cross over the bridge" connecting the bluff of "segregation" to the opposite side. The man, his hands behind his back, perhaps because he doesn't want to be pulled across the bridge, is reluctant to step on the rickety structure. In a similar vein, a cartoon published by Jon Kennedy in the *Little Rock* (Ark.) *Democrat* represents the South as making "steady progress" ploughing the field of "race relations"

'Gone With the Wind'

"CROSS OVER THE BRIDGE"

behind the workhorse of "Gradualism." However, a judge, leading a thoroughbred named "Forced Progress," complains that the South is "not going fast enough." The caption reads "No Job For A Race Horse."

Though the Supreme Court declared segregation of public schools unconstitutional in May 1954, it declined to issue any specific enforcement order, scheduling the matter for re-argument the following year. At the re-argument, lawyers for the National Association for the Advancement of Colored People (NAACP), the civil rights organization that for decades had led the fight for integrated public schools, argued that desegregation should commence immediately and comprehensively throughout the South, while the southern states supported a slow gradual approach that took into account "local conditions." In its decision that it handed down in 1955, the Court opted for gradualism. It remanded the five cases consolidated in *Brown* to the federal district courts and ordered them to

admit the parties of the cases "to the public schools on a racially non-discriminatory basis with all deliberate speed." A cartoon published by Cal Alley in the *Memphis Commercial Appeal* alludes to this ruling. It shows a startled figure—the Federal District Courts—juggling the "hot potato" of desegregation while the Supreme Court walks away in the background. Probably Alley is charging that the Court is not giving the lower federal district courts enough guidance on how they are to enforce the *Brown* decision.

Perhaps emboldened by the Supreme Court's decision not to require immediate and total desegregation, many southern states delayed desegregating their public schools. One of the more infamous of these efforts occurred in Little Rock, Arkansas, in September 1957. Governor Orval Faubus called out the Arkansas National Guard to stop nine African-American children from attending Central High School. He justified his actions by claiming that public disorder would be imminent if black children were to attend the all-white institution. After a federal judge forced Faubus to withdraw the Guard, a mob of segregationists prevented the black children from entering the school. To restore order, President Eisenhower sent in federal troops and declared martial law. The local federal district judge granted a request by local school officials to delay desegregation of Central High for two and a half years. The NAACP appealed to the Supreme Court, which unanimously ruled in *Cooper v. Aaron* (1958) that Central High had to be desegregated immediately and that state officials had an obligation to respect the Court's decision in *Brown*. The atmosphere of the times is captured in a cartoon published by Yardley in the *Baltimore Sun*. It shows a determined Deep South segregationist going "nose to nose" with the Supreme Court. The Court says desegregate "NOW," but the segregationist, a bottle of "Ol Faubus" in his pocket, refuses to submit. The caption reads, "An immovable object meets an irresistible force."

Despite the Court's ruling in *Cooper v. Aaron*, the slow pace of desegregation continued. Real progress did not occur until after Martin Luther King and other black leaders ushered in the civil rights movement of the 1960s. The sit-in demonstrations in private restaurants, the large freedom marches in southern cities, the rise of Malcolm X and his open advocacy of black revolution—all of these together convinced President John F. Kennedy and many of his allies in Congress that the federal government had to do more to ease racial tension, both in the South and the North. Following Kennedy's assassination in November 1963, support for his proposal grew, and the Civil Rights Act of 1964 was enacted in June of that year. This law prohibited private discrimination in public accommodations. No longer could private hotels, motels, restaurants, theaters, concert halls, or any other facility that served the

"An immovable object meets an irresistible force."

public discriminate against an individual on the basis of "race, color, religion, or national origin." In addition, one of the law's provisions gave the attorney general the power to file suits against public schools that refused to desegregate. The federal government could now become directly involved in the fight for desegregated schools.

In 1966, the Department of Health, Education, and Welfare issued "guidelines" spelling out what a school district had to achieve before the department would consider it desegregated. Nonracial attendance zones or freedom-of-choice plans that let parents choose what schools their children would attend were not enough. Before the department would recognize a school district as desegregated, a significant number of African-American students had to attend formerly all-white schools, and a significant number of white students had to attend formerly all-black schools. To avoid a possible lawsuit initiated by the federal government, a southern school district therefore had to integrate its schools. Local federal courts quickly adopted these definitions and the issue of mandatory integration came before the Supreme Court in *Green v. County Board of New Kent County* (1968). The school board argued that desegregation had been achieved on the basis of a freedom-of-choice plan, even though relatively few black students attended the formerly all-white school and no white students attended the all-black school. The Supreme Court disagreed, holding that the school board had an "affirmative duty" to create a "unitary system in which racial discrimination would be eliminated root and branch." The Court added that the "burden on a school board today is to come forward with a plan that promises realistically to work, and promises realistically to work *now*." The italicized "now" was a sign that the Court's patience, fourteen years after *Brown*, had finally come to an end. Southern school districts were now under a legal obligation, not to desegregate their schools "with all deliberate speed," but to integrate them immediately.

In the presidential election of 1968, Republican nominee Richard Nixon sympathized with southern concerns about court-ordered integration of public schools. Pursuing his so-called southern strategy, Nixon successfully split the Democratic Party in the South and won the election. Soon thereafter, his

administration requested the Court of Appeals for the Fifth Circuit to delay issuing a desegregation plan for Mississippi until December 1, 1969. On August 28, the Fifth Circuit granted the request, but the NAACP appealed. In *Alexander v. Holmes County Board of Education* (1969), the Supreme Court reversed the lower court's decision, ruling that every school district was under an obligation "to terminate dual school systems at once and to operate now and hereafter only unitary schools." The result is humorously depicted in a cartoon that Jerry Fearing drew for the *St. Paul Dispatch*. A puzzled Richard Nixon is sadly eyeing Chief Justice Warren Burger, who has just popped an advocate of "Go Slow On Integration" on the

'I Thought You Said the Judge and You Were Just Like That'

head with his "Integrate At Once" gavel. The man, lying on the floor with his head smarting, crosses his fingers and says to Nixon, "I thought you said the judge and you were just like that." Burger, whom Nixon had appointed Chief Justice after Earl Warren's resignation in June 1969, had a reputation as a conservative judge who opposed judicial activism. The amusing caption reflects the fact that presidents are at times surprised and disappointed by their appointments to the Supreme Court.

A couple of years later, in *Swann v. Charlotte-Mecklenburg Board of Education* (1971), a unanimous decision, Burger outlined what lower federal judges could do to achieve immediate racial integration of public schools. Underlining the broad equitable powers of these judges, Burger insisted that they could not only redraw attendance zones, outlaw predominantly one-race schools, and use racial quotas to achieve proper racial balances in individual schools, but they could also order extensive busing of school children. Opposition to busing grew steadily during the 1970s, especially after a Supreme Court decision significantly widened the scope of busing. The *Swann* decision had meant that lower federal judges could order busing only in those states that had mandated or authorized segregation by *law*. In *Keyes v. Denver School District No. 1* (1973), however, the Court held that a federal judge could use the equitable remedies described in *Swann,* including busing, to force the school district of Denver to integrate, even though Colorado had never mandated or authorized segregation. The Court based its decision on the fact that local school officials in part of Denver's district had purposefully kept black and white children in separate schools. Such intentional discrimination by school officials was as unlawful as segregation by law. The implication was that federal judges could order busing in any northern school district that had pursued policies of segregated education anytime after 1954. *Keyes* therefore made many large urban school districts in the North vulnerable to court-ordered busing.

A cartoon published in the *Sunday Star* captured the irony of the situation. It shows Chief Justice Burger commanding a Northern schoolchild into the "washtub" of the desegregation decision. The hot water, the soap, and the stiff brush that Burger is holding in his right hand all suggest that the untidy youth is in for a painful experience. In the background, a well-scrubbed youngster draped in a Confederate flag smirks in satisfaction at what awaits his counterpart, reflecting the fact that by this time many southern school districts had achieved a significant degree of racial integration. The transformation had not been easy or complete. In many parts of the South, white parents pulled their children out of the public schools and sent them to segregated private academies. Nevertheless, by 1973 many public schools in the South were in fact more integrated than those in either the North or the West.

Following the Court's decision in *Keyes,* federal judges ordered one northern city after another to integrate its schools. Busing became widespread and public opposition to it grew. Many white parents, rather than let their children be bused to an integrated school across town, moved out of the cities to the suburbs. The cities became more and more concentrated with minority populations, some to the point that there were not enough whites left in the school district to achieve any meaningful racial integration. The result was that the former system or practice of *de jure* segregation (segregation by law or by the decisions of school officials) gradually gave way to the reality of *de facto* segregation (segregation by housing). In Detroit, a federal judge tried to counter the trend by ordering inter-district remedies for *de jure* segregation that had taken place in the city's school district. To achieve meaningful integration in the city, the judge ordered black children from Detroit bussed to schools in the white suburbs and white children from the suburbs bussed to schools in the city. In *Milliken v. Bradley* (1974), the Supreme Court reversed the lower federal judge's decision, ruling that intra-district violations only merited intra-district remedies. As long as the suburban school districts had not participated in the constitutional violation, they could not be made to remedy the constitutional wrong. It's arguable that in *Milliken* the Court bowed to political pressure. The unfortunate result, however, is that the percentage of black children attending truly integrated schools is today not much higher than it was in 1968. ⚖

'In you go!'

Prayer in Public Schools

CHAPTER 13

Prayer in Public Schools

Prayer in public schools was common in the United States until the Supreme Court declared it unconstitutional in 1962. Prior to then, the Court had avoided the issue of school prayer, though it had decided a number of related matters. For example, in *Everson v. Board of Education* (1947), though the Court proclaimed that the Establishment Clause of the First Amendment "was intended to erect a 'wall of separation' between Church and State," it nonetheless upheld the practice of providing public bus transportation to children attending parochial as well as public schools. A year later, in *McCollum v. Board of Education* the Court significantly raised the "wall" separating church and state by invalidating an Illinois law that permitted religious groups to use public classrooms to teach religion during school hours. Proponents of school prayer attacked the decision vehemently, arguing that it undercut the religious education of the nation's youth. On March 11, 1948, a cartoon drawn by Jim Berryman for the *Washington Star* expressed what many Americans were feeling in reaction to the Court's decision in *McCollum*. It shows the Supreme Court, represented as a blindfolded robed figure posing as Emperor Napoleon, holding a scale of justice that is measuring the Holy Bible against the "U.S. Constitution" and "Atheism." Berryman's association of the latter two books strongly suggests that he thought *McCollum* was unjustifiably hostile to religion. In any case, in *Zorach v. Clausen* (1952), the Court adopted a more accommodating attitude towards reli-

gion by upholding New York City's "released time" program for religious instruction. Though religious instruction could not be conducted on public school grounds, a public school could cooperate with religious groups by letting children receive religious instruction during school hours as long as the instruction took place off school property.

Though these three decisions did not specifically deal with prayer in public schools, they strongly hinted that a sectarian prayer was unconstitutional because it meant that a public school was preferring one religion over others, thereby violating the "wall of separation" that the Court had established in *Everson.* Accordingly, to avoid offending the Establishment Clause, public officials in New York formulated a "nonsectarian" prayer: "Almighty God, we acknowledge our dependence upon Thee, and we beg Thy blessing upon us, our parents, our teachers, and our Country." Though the students could decide for themselves whether to pray or not, teachers in New York led the prayer and the prayer occurred during the school day. Civil libertarians argued that such a state-authored prayer was yet unconstitutional because it involved state support for religion over nonreligion. Defenders of the law emphasized that the law was non-coercive and that no religion was receiving any public money. In *Engel v. Vitale* (1962), the Supreme Court ruled that even such a non-sectarian prayer in public schools was an unconstitutional establishment of religion. In the words of the majority opinion by Justice Hugo Black, having public school teachers encourage students to pray was "a practice wholly inconsistent with the Establishment Clause."

The Court's ruling in *Engel* caused a huge public outcry and cartoonists took opposing sides on whether the Supreme Court had acted properly. In a cartoon he drew for the *Chicago Sun-Times,* Ed Burck endorsed the decision as God's "11th Commandment," thereby implying that a vigorous enforcement of the Establishment Clause was divinely ordained and in the best interests of all religions. In contrast, Alexander drew a cartoon for the *Philadelphia Bulletin* captioned "Segregated." It shows the Supreme Court finishing a sign barring "The Deity" from a public school while a little schoolboy looks on. Indirectly alluding to the fact that the Supreme Court had compelled public

The 11th Commandment

schools to admit African Americans, the cartoon seems to be hinting that the Court has no business keeping God out. In any case, by placing the issue of school prayer into the context of desegregation, Alexander's cartoon reflects the intensity of the public's reaction. In the eyes of the American public, *Engel* was one of the more controversial decisions the Court had made since *Brown v. Board of Education.*

The following year, in *School District of Abington Township v. Schempp,* the Supreme Court struck down a Pennsylvania law requiring teachers in all public schools to read "at least ten verses from the Holy Bible" each day. The ruling deepened the impression that the Court was interpreting the Establishment

SEGREGATED

Clause to forbid the state from not only preferring one religion over another, but also from providing any support to religion in general. Cartoonists had a field day probing what the rulings in *Engel* and *Schempp* would mean if carried to their logical extreme. Must "God" be taken out of the pledge of allegiance? The nation's motto "In God We Trust"? The Supreme Court's traditional opening chant that calls on God to "save the United States and this honorable court"? Of course, the Court has never extended its decisions on school prayer to these extreme results. For example, in *Marsh v. Chambers* (1983) the Court upheld the Nebraska legislature's tradition of opening each legislative day with a prayer by a chaplain paid by the state.

Over the years, opposition to the Supreme Court's decisions on prayer and Bible reading in public schools produced periodic attempts to pass a constitutional amendment that would protect voluntary school prayer and other forms of religious activities in public schools. President Ronald Reagan, in particular, supported such an effort during his term of office in the 1980s. On March 6, 1984, a cartoon by Tom Flannery appeared in the *Baltimore Sun* that mocks this attempt to carve an exception to the Establishment Clause. It depicts two men, who symbolize Congress, reviewing the Constitution in the light passing through a stained glass window. Referring to the school prayer amendment, one says to the other, "We can stick it in right about here." The impression left by the cartoon is that Congress was trying to put something into the Constitution that did not belong there. Rightly or wrongly, opponents of school prayer were always able to garner the support needed to defeat any attempt in Congress to pass a school prayer amendment. However, the inability of the conservatives to pass a constitutional amendment did not mean that school prayer disappeared from all American public classrooms. Across

"WE CAN STICK IT IN RIGHT ABOUT HERE"

'Since The Government Gave Its OK, We're Going
To Hold A Worship Service In Room 215 Today'

the country, many local communities, in particular those that were religiously homogeneous, have refused to comply with the Court's ruling outlawing prayer in public schools.

In *Widmar v. Vincent* (1981), the Supreme Court decided that a state university which made its facilities available for use by student groups could not discriminate against groups on the basis of their ideology. Such discrimination involved content-based restrictions that violated freedom of speech. In other words, freedom of speech required equal access to all student organizations, including those that were completely or predominantly religious in character. In 1984, Congress built upon the *Widmar* decision by enacting the Equal Access Act. This law required any primary or secondary school receiving federal financial assistance not to deny access to any school group on the basis of its religious, political, or philosophical outlook if the school allowed any student group to meet on school property outside regular school hours. Tom Engelhardt pokes fun at one scenario of this legislation in a cartoon that appeared in the *St. Louis Post-Dispatch*. A group of students well outside the religious mainstream—one carrying a snake, another a drum, and yet another holding up a skull—enter a principal's office and inform him that they going to hold a worship service in Room 215!

The Supreme Court upheld the Equal Access Act in *Board of Education v. Mergens* (1990), holding that it did not violate the Establishment Clause if a public school allowed a group of students to read the Bible and pray together after school hours on school property as long as the school permitted other student groups the same degree of access to its facilities. A cartoon drawn by Walt Handelsman for the *New Orleans Times-Picayune* provides a humorous explanation for the Court's decision in *Mergens*. A youngster suggests to a friend that the

justices changed course on prayer in public schools because student test scores had fallen. Though it's true that throughout the 1980s test scores of American students fell, there's no truth to the cartoon's amusing insinuation. The Court permitted student groups to pray after school on the ground of freedom of speech and the right of students to exercise freely the religion of their choice, not as a strategy to elevate student test scores.

After it became clear that a constitutional amendment authorizing school prayer would never get through Congress, many state legislatures in the early 1980s passed laws requiring a moment of silence at the beginning of each school day, during which time a student could pray, meditate, or daydream. The constitutionality of such measures was hotly debated in the public media and commentators argued among themselves whether the Supreme Court would uphold or strike down the practice. In a cartoon he drew for the *Seattle Post-Intelligencer* in 1984, David Horsey provides a scathing visualization of the Court pondering whether a moment of silence law is constitutional or not. A little boy is sitting at his desk with his head lying on his folded hands. Staring intently at him are four justices of the Supreme Court, three of whom claim that the boy is praying, but the fourth discovers that he's not. "No. He's snoring." Horsey may well be suggesting that the Court would be

wasting its time trying to fathom the religious significance of children beginning their school day with a moment of silence.

Despite the tone of Horsey's cartoon, the Supreme Court took up the moment-of-silence issue the following year in *Wallace v. Jaffree*. The case concerned an Alabama law that authorized a one-minute period of silence at the start of each school day "for meditation or voluntary prayer." The law was an amendment of an earlier Alabama statute that had authorized a moment of silence "for meditation." The Court ruled that the new law was unconstitutional because it was "not motivated by any secular purpose." It was rather a deliberate attempt to return voluntary prayer to the schools under the cover of a moment of silence. In her concurrence, Justice Sandra Day O'Connor emphasized that a moment of silence would be constitutional if the law in question did not endorse or sponsor prayer. Chief Justice Warren Burger and Justices Byron White and William Rehnquist dissented.

In 1986, the Supreme Court ruled in *Bethel School District No. 403 v. Fraser* that freedom of speech did not prevent a public school from disciplining a high school student for giving a lewd speech at a school assembly. In a nomination speech that he gave for one of his fellow students, Matthew Fraser had made ample use of sexual innuendos, which titillated some of

the six hundred students listening, but embarrassed and bewildered others. Wayne Skayskal took this decision as an opportunity to draw a cartoon that contrasted Justice O'Connor's suggestion that a moment of silence could be constitutional with the Court's ruling in *Fraser*. In the cartoon's background, a current-events board announces that the Supreme Court has limited the free speech rights of students. In the foreground, a crabby old teacher admonishes a student that he can't have a moment of silent vulgarity. The idea that students might be using the moment of silence to think impure thoughts is a particularly droll comment on the kind of tension that can arise between the Establishment Clause and freedom of speech.

In more recent years, the Supreme Court has maintained its tradition of opposing officially-sanctioned prayer on school grounds. In *Lee v. Weissman* (1992), the Court ruled in a 5 to 4 decision that a school district could not invite members of the clergy to deliver nonsectarian prayers at a school's graduation ceremony. Even if students were not required to attend graduation to receive their diplomas, the Court said that the practice was unconstitutional because it amounted to state-sponsored prayer. On June 19, 2000, in *Santa Fe v. Doe,* a 6 to 3 decision, the Court invalidated a Texas school district's policy that authorized the delivery of an "invocation or message" by a high school student before home varsity football games. Though students of the school decided whether to have these invocations and elected the spokesperson who would deliver them, the Court nonetheless ruled that they were public rather than private speeches. Because the speeches were authorized by a government policy that encouraged religious messages and because they took place on government property at a government-sponsored sporting event, they constituted a public endorsement of religion and therefore violated the Establishment Clause. These two decisions make it relatively clear that the Court is not likely to retreat any time soon from its firm stand against school prayer.

CHAPTER 14

Watergate and Executive Privilege

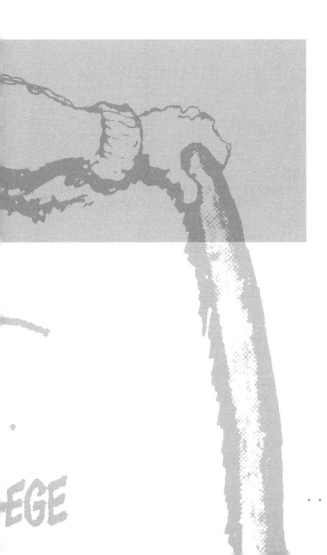

On June 17, 1972, the police arrested five men for breaking into the offices of the Democratic National Committee at the Watergate Complex in Washington, D.C. It was quickly discovered that one of the five, James McCord, was the security coordinator for the Committee to Re-elect the President (CREEP). Eventually, many of Nixon's top aides were implicated in the break-in and the cover-up that followed. One of these aides, John Dean, testified before a Senate Select Committee that the president himself had participated in the cover-up. There didn't seem to be any chance that Dean's allegation could be corroborated until it was discovered that Nixon had taped his presidential conversations. Claiming executive privilege, Nixon refused to hand the tapes over to either Congress or the courts. In *United States v. Nixon* (1974), the Supreme Court considered whether Nixon had the right to ignore a judicial subpoena for the tapes. The Court's decision played a pivotal role in determining Nixon's fate and resolving a major constitutional crisis.

The Watergate break-in was at first viewed as a third-rate burglary. Untainted by the break-in, Nixon won a landslide victory over his Democratic rival George McGovern in the November 1972 presidential election. Soon after his second inauguration, however, Nixon and his administration came under increasingly sharp attacks. In January 1973, the trial of the Watergate burglars uncovered evidence that high White House officials had tried to

I WANT **YOUR** TAPES

FOR THE SENATE WATERGATE COMMITTEE

impede the Federal Bureau of Investigation inquiry into who had ordered the break-in. In February, the Senate created a select committee, with North Carolina Senator Sam Ervin as its chair, to examine the Watergate affair and other illegal and unethical activities that had occurred during the 1972 election. In May, Attorney General Elliot Richardson named Archibald Cox, a Harvard law professor who had been solicitor general during the Kennedy administration, special prosecutor in charge of the ongoing criminal investigation. The following month, John Dean testified before the Senate Watergate Committee that President Nixon was an active participant in the cover-up of the break-in. John Mitchell, CREEP director and Nixon's former attorney general; H. R. Haldeman, Nixon's

chief of staff; and John Ehrlichman, director of the Domestic Council, all of whom by this time had resigned their positions, denied Dean's allegations. The situation was one of stalemate, with Nixon, Mitchell, Haldeman, and Ehrlichman on one side and the soft-spoken, unflappable Dean on the other.

Then, on July 16, Alexander Butterfield, an aide to Haldeman, startled the entire country by testifying that Nixon had taped all of his presidential conversations in the Oval Office. Everyone immediately realized that the tapes could either clear Nixon or expose him. The Senate Watergate Committee issued a congressional subpoena for the tapes, which became the subject of a cartoon drawn by Robert Graysmith for the *San Francisco Chronicle*. Playing upon a familiar ad for military service, it features Sam Ervin dressed up as Uncle Sam pointing his finger at the viewer and saying "I Want YOUR Tapes," instead of "I Want YOU." Ervin's committee, however, never got the tapes. After Nixon invoked executive privilege, the committee took Nixon to court, but District Judge Gerhard Gesell declined to enforce the congressional subpoena. In his judgment, Nixon's interest in keeping executive information confidential was more important than the committee's need for the tapes.

Despite Judge Gesell's decision, Nixon's troubles continued to mount. In July, Cox convinced Judge Sirica, the federal district judge who had presided over the trial of the Watergate burglars, that nine of Nixon's tapes were relevant to the grand jury's criminal investigation of who authorized the Watergate break-in and participated in the attempt to cover it up. The judge issued a subpoena for the tapes, but Nixon again claimed executive privilege and appealed to the Court of Appeals in Washington, D.C. The irony was that a president who had always portrayed himself as a proponent of law and order appeared to be using the doctrine of executive privilege as a shield to protect his subordinates from criminal prosecution. A cartoon drawn by Doug Marlette for the *Charlotte* (N.C.) *Observer* comments on this theme. It depicts Nixon as a sweating "Law-and-Order-Man" who is using his cape of executive privilege to hide from view three individuals, presumably Mitchell, Haldeman, and Ehrlichman. At his feet are a Watergate tape machine, a stack of hush money, and a bag of plumber's tools. (The latter is a reference to a special White House investigation unit [called "the plumbers"] that Nixon had created in 1971 to stop security leaks and investigate sensitive national security matters.) "Law-and-Order-Man" was therefore using executive privilege to hide, not just the Watergate break-in, but a whole series of illegal acts, including unlawful wiretaps and burglaries.

' "Goodness gracious," cried Dick. "The tapes! They've disappeared!" '

In October, the Court of Appeals decided, 5 to 2, that presidential conversations were "presumptively privileged," but that Nixon nonetheless had to turn over the nine tapes to Cox and the grand jury. At this point, Nixon could have appealed to the Supreme Court. Instead, on October 20, he ordered Attorney General Richardson to fire Cox. The result was the infamous Saturday Night Massacre. Rather than dismiss Cox, Richardson and his deputy William Ruckelshaus resigned. Nixon thereupon appointed Solicitor General Robert Bork acting attorney general and ordered him to discharge Cox. Bork obeyed and FBI agents occupied the offices of Richardson, Ruckelshaus, and Cox. It appeared that Nixon was trying to take personal control of an investigation that had uncovered him as a suspect.

The public's reaction was adamant. In response to protestors marching with signs asking drivers to "Honk for Impeachment,"

car horns blared in front of the White House. A flood of telegrams poured into Washington. Politicians, newspaper editorials, TV commentators, and public interest groups condemned Cox's dismissal, demanded that the tapes be turned over to the grand jury, and called for Nixon's resignation or impeachment. Facing this degree of opposition, Nixon retreated and agreed to deliver the nine subpoenaed tapes to Judge Sirica. Ten days later, however, the White House announced that two of the tapes were missing. On November 2, 1973, a cartoon by Jeff MacNelly appeared in *The Richmond* (Va.) *News Leader* that humorously speculates on Judge Sirica's reaction to the news of the missing tapes. The cartoon shows Mother Goose reading to Judge Sirica a fairy tale in which "Dick" announces that the tapes have disappeared. The tossed gavel and the expression on Sirica's face, his eyes uplifted in disbelief, indirectly reflect the American public's increasingly skeptical attitude toward Nixon.

A few weeks after the announcement of the two missing tapes, another incredible revelation came out of the White House. There was an eighteen-minute gap in the tape of a conversation that Nixon had with Haldeman three days after the Watergate break-in. All that one could hear on the tape was a loud hum. On November 26, Rose Mary Woods, the president's personal secretary, testified under oath that she caused the gap when she answered a phone call while she was transcribing the tapes. She claimed that she must have pressed the "record" button on the tape recorder rather than the "stop" button. But since the tape recorder would have turned off unless a foot pedal had been depressed throughout the phone conversation, Woods's explanation of the gap was not very convincing. In a courtroom demonstration, Woods attempted to keep the recorder's foot pedal depressed and answer the phone at the same time (a feat which became known as "the Rose Mary stretch"), but she was unable to do so. Dick Locher cleverly mocks Woods's credibility in a cartoon he drew for the *Chicago Tribune.* Asked about the "Nixon-Dean recording," Woods says, "Give me the first few bars . . . and I'll HUM eighteen minutes of it." The cartoon's not-so-subtle suggestion is that Woods had tampered with the tapes.

Given the hostility of the public's reaction to Cox's dismissal, Nixon had no choice but to appoint a new special prosecutor. He chose Leon Jaworski, a lawyer from Texas who had been a friend of Lyndon Johnson and a former president of the American Bar Association. Before taking the job, Jaworski got assurances from Alexander Haig, Nixon's new chief of staff, that he could take the president to court and that he could not be discharged (absent extraordinary improprieties) without the approval of eight prominent congressional leaders. Jaworski prosecuted the case vigorously.

'Hey, wait a minute . . . I hired you to clean up the place, but this is ridiculous'

EXECUTIVE PRIVILEGE

JAWORSKI SPECIAL PROSECUTOR

On March 1, 1974, a grand jury indicted all of Nixon's top lieutenants, including Mitchell, Haldeman, and Ehrlichman, for conspiracy to obstruct justice and other crimes. Nixon was not indicted, but that was only because Jaworski doubted that he could constitutionally indict a sitting president. The grand jury nonetheless secretly named Nixon as an unindicted co-conspirator and submitted a sealed report to Sirica summarizing the evidence against him. Having laid this groundwork, Jaworski successfully obtained a subpoena for an additional sixty-four tapes of Nixon's conversations in the Oval Office. Guernsey Le Pelley drew a cartoon for the *Christian Science Monitor* that focused on Nixon's reaction to Jaworski's relentless probe. Holding the scales of executive privilege, Nixon peeks out from under his blindfold and admonishes Jaworski, who is scrubbing the floor under Nixon's robe, "Hey, wait a minute . . . I hired you to clean up the place, but this is ridiculous."

Nixon appealed Judge Sirica's subpoena to the Court of Appeals. Time was on Nixon's side. Even if he lost at the Court of Appeals, he could take his claim of executive privilege to the Supreme Court. The longer he could delay a final decision, the more likely it was that the House Judiciary Committee would have to vote on whether to recommend Nixon's impeachment to the full House without the benefit of the tapes. Jaworski countered by convincing the Supreme Court to postpone its summer recess and invoke a rarely used procedure by which a case can bypass the Court of Appeals and come immediately before the high court. Justice William H. Rehnquist, who was appointed to the Court by Nixon, excused himself from the case because he had earlier worked in the Department of Justice under John Mitchell. Three of the remaining eight justices were also Nixon appointees: Chief Justice Warren Burger, Justice Harry A. Blackmun, and

'. . . Hi ya, Warren, how's the wife? . . . Potter, you ol' rattlesnake, what's new? . . .
Thurgood, ol' buddy, long time no . . .'

Justice Lewis F. Powell Jr. Mike Peters drew a cartoon for the *Dayton Daily News* that highlighted Nixon's personal relationships with the eight justices who were going to decide whether he had to comply with the judicial subpoena. After asking Warren Burger how his wife is and what's new with Potter Stewart, a squirrelly Nixon exclaims, "Long time no . . . ," to his "buddy" Thurgood Marshall, a former head of the NAACP's Legal Defense Fund and the first African American appointed to the Supreme Court. Nixon doesn't finish the greeting, which is amusing because he and Marshall were from opposite ends of the political spectrum and were far from being friends of any sort. The cartoon raises the interesting question, however, whether personal relationships ever have an impact on decisions of the Supreme Court.

The Supreme Court decided *United States v. Nixon* very quickly. On July 24, sixteen days after oral argument, on the very day that the House Judiciary Committee began its public debate on the articles of impeachment, the Court unanimously ruled that, though executive privilege was constitutionally rooted, it was not an absolute right. It was rather a qualified right subject to judicial scrutiny on a case-by-case basis. Since Nixon was asserting only a generalized interest in confidentiality, while Jaworski had established a specific need for the evidence in a criminal trial, Nixon had to turn over the sixty-four tapes to Judge Sirica so that he could review them and rule on whether the conversations were admissible and relevant. As a cartoon drawn by Le Pelley for *The Christian Science Monitor* pictured it, the Court had rapped the doctrine of executive privilege with its gavel so hard that Nixon and his tapes were left high and dry with no place to go.

At this point, Nixon could either disobey the Supreme Court decision or deliver the tapes to Judge Sirica. There was some

'On second thought...'

As it was, by July 30, the House Judiciary Committee recommended three articles of impeachment to the full House of Representatives. These articles charged Nixon with obstruction of justice, abuse of presidential power, and non-compliance with the committee's subpoenas. On August 5, Nixon announced that he planned to make public transcripts of three conversations that he had with Haldeman on June 23, 1972, six days after the break-in. He admitted that these transcripts "may further damage" his case, but he asked that they be understood "in perspective." In fact, the transcripts doomed Nixon's presidency because they conclusively showed that Nixon had obstructed justice by ordering the Central Intelligence Agency to block the FBI investigation into the Watergate break-in and that he had lied to the American people about his involvement in the cover-up from the very beginning. A cartoon drawn by Ed Gamble for the *Nashville Banner* figuratively captures Nixon's predicament. After "stonewalling" for years, Nixon can no longer keep the waters of impeachment from lapping over the walls of his little island. His only option is to get into the raft of resignation. Nixon in fact took this step on August 9, 1974, becoming the first president to resign from the nation's highest office.

speculation that Nixon might ignore the Court's decision because in an earlier public statement he had said that he would obey only a "definitive" ruling by the Court. Finally, after several hours, Nixon's lawyer appeared on television and indicated that the president was going to comply with the Court's unanimous decision "in all respects." A cartoon by Art Poinier that appeared in the *Detroit News* underscored the prudential character of Nixon's decision not to disobey the Court's ruling. It shows a tiny Nixon climbing into a boxing ring with a giant Supreme Court, having a "second thought," and climbing right back out again. It is very likely that Nixon would have been impeached and convicted if he had ignored the Supreme Court's order to turn over the tapes to Judge Sirica.

CHAPTER 15

Abortion

In 1969, Norma McCorvey filed suit against Texas, claiming that the law which prevented her from getting an abortion was unconstitutional. At the time, only four states allowed abortions: New York, Hawaii, Alaska, and Washington. Her case—which became known as *Roe v. Wade*—eventually wound up at the Supreme Court, where it simmered for more than a year as the justices struggled to find the proper balance between a woman's right to choose and a fetus's right to life. Finally, on January 22, 1973, the Supreme Court ruled 7 to 2 that a woman has a right to an abortion, but the right was qualified, depending on the stage of pregnancy: during the first trimester, a woman could have an abortion at her discretion; during the second, a state could regulate abortions in the interest of the health of the mother; during the third, a state could prohibit abortions for the sake of the potential life of the fetus.

Though *Roe* limited a woman's right to have an abortion, the pro-choice movement quickly proclaimed it a victory. Opposition to the decision coalesced around the Catholic Church, which unleashed a massive lobbying effort to pass a constitutional amendment outlawing abortion. In 1974, four American cardinals (Timothy Manning, Humberto Medeiros, John Krol, and John Cody) testified in favor of an amendment before a Senate subcommittee—the first time a cardinal had ever testified at a congressional hearing. Their effort to pass such an amendment, however, proved fruitless. In the presidential election of 1976, Jimmy Carter promised only that he would not

THE JUDGMENT OF SOLOMON

work "to block" a pro-life amendment, while President Gerald Ford favored an amendment that would only transfer the issue to the states, letting each state decide for itself under what conditions, if any, it would allow abortions. However, no pro-life amendment of any type ever gained the requisite two-thirds majority of either house of Congress. An attempt to bypass Congress with a constitutional convention also fell short. By 1978, only thirteen state legislatures had voted in favor of a convention, twenty-one shy of the thirty-four legislatures needed to convene such an assembly.

The pro-life movement was more successful at eliminating public financing of abortions through Medicaid, the cooperative federal-state program that provides medical services to the poor. In *Maher v. Roe* (1977), the Supreme Court upheld a Connecticut law that eliminated Medicaid funding for "medically unnecessary" abortions. Draper Hill drew a cartoon for

the *Detroit News* that sarcastically referred to the decision as "the judgment of Solomon." Armed with the sword of the *Maher* ruling, the Court cuts a symbolic woman into a rich half that yet has an effective right to an abortion and a poor half that does not. At the federal level, Republican Henry Hyde, a freshman congressman from Illinois, led the fight to eliminate Medicaid funding for abortions except "where the life of the mother would be endangered." The harsher federal restriction came up for review in *Harris v. McRae* (1980). In this 6 to 3 decision, the Court concluded once again that a pregnant woman has a constitutional right to an abortion, but not to one paid for by government. Accordingly, a poor woman whose pregnancy was not life-threatening could either carry the baby to term and have all the expenses of delivery covered by Medicaid or pay for her own abortion if she could find some means to finance it.

Though the Supreme Court accepted limitations on publicly funded abortions, it invalidated other types of restrictions during the 1970s and 1980s. For example, the Court threw out state laws mandating that all second-trimester abortions be done in hospitals, compelling doctors to inform pregnant women of the development of the fetus and the complications that could result from an abortion, and requiring a woman to obtain her husband's consent prior to an abortion. However, laws requiring a juvenile to obtain the consent of her parents were upheld if they contained a so-called "judicial bypass," a procedure by which a pregnant juvenile could get an abortion without parental permission if she could show a judge either that she was competent to make the decision or that an abortion was in her best interest.

By the mid-1980s, President Ronald Reagan's appointments to the Supreme Court had changed its complexion significantly. The two original dissenters in *Roe*—Chief Justice William H. Rehnquist and Justice Byron White—had gained two apparent allies: Justices Sandra Day O'Connor and Antonin Scalia. They needed only one more justice to reverse *Roe*. In 1987, Reagan ratcheted up the political tension by nominating Robert Bork, a known critic of *Roe*, to fill the seat left vacant when Justice Lewis Powell, an abortion rights supporter, resigned. A bruising nomination battle followed, ending with Bork's defeat by a vote of 42 to 58. Reagan subsequently nominated and the Senate confirmed Judge Anthony Kennedy, a moderate who claimed during his confirmation hearing that he had "no fixed view" on the issue of abortion. A year later, a major abortion decision, *Webster v. Reproductive Services* (1989), came before the Court. Anticipating that *Roe* was about to be overturned, the National Association for the Repeal of Abortion Laws (NARAL) unleashed a major publicity campaign to re-energize the pro-choice movement.

A cartoon by Tom Toles, which appeared in the *Buffalo News* on January 25, 1989, commented on the Court's predicament. Though the cartoon says that the justices are engaged in "difficult legal research on the abortion case," what it shows them doing is studying a weather vane, presumably to detect which way the political wind is blowing. The comment at the bottom-right corner, "Gusty up here," is a reflection on the political

factors that can sometimes influence Supreme Court decisions. A week before *Webster* was argued before the Supreme Court, John Slade drew a cartoon for the *Louisiana Weekly* that relied on military metaphors to dramatize the unyielding character of the opposition between the pro-life and pro-choice movements. Two tanks face off in front of the Supreme Court, each refusing to give ground, just as each side of the abortion controversy refused to accept significant compromises.

The Missouri law under review in *Webster* required physicians to perform specific tests to determine viability if the fetus was approximately twenty or more weeks old, prohibited public facilities from performing abortions not endangering the life of the woman, the use of any public funds to "counsel" a woman to have an abortion, and proclaimed that life began at conception. In a 5 to 4 decision, the Court upheld each of these provisions without explicitly overturning *Roe v. Wade*. In a cartoon he published in 1989, Jim Borgman for the *Cincinnati Enquirer* poked fun at the Court's ruling. Nine old justices, some asleep, all morose and tired looking, decide that life begins, not at

Still white hot. . .

THAT'S IT, THEN? WE'RE GOING WITH THAT? LIFE BEGINS AT 40?

SUPREME COURT

conception, but at forty. Such an absurd ruling, Borgman seems to be saying, was no more sensible than what the Court had said in *Webster*.

Because *Webster* left *Roe* intact, though, as it was often said, "hanging by a thread," members of the Senate Judiciary Committee understandably tried to find out how new nominees to the Supreme Court would vote on abortion. David Souter, nominated by President George Bush in 1990, faced fierce questioning, in part because his predecessor, Justice William Brennan, had been a member of the *Roe* majority and a stalwart defender of a woman's right to choose. The feeling was that if Souter got on the Court and joined the *Webster* majority, *Roe* would be endangered. During his confirmation hearings, however, Souter followed Kennedy's example. He deflected one question after another on abortion and assured senators that he had no "agenda" or "rigid jurisprudence." Jim Berry parodied Souter's performance in a cartoon he drew for the *Washington Times* on August 13, 1990. It pictured Souter as the Cheshire Cat in *Alice in Wonderland*. Alice asks him how he stands on abortion, but the cat just smiles in reply. Though his evasive answers

did not win him the support of the National Organization for Women (NOW), the Planned Parenthood Federation of America, and other prominent pro-choice groups, Souter's tactic proved effective. He won confirmation by a vote of 90 to 9.

Justice Souter's first vote in an abortion case did nothing to relieve the anxieties of the pro-choice movement. In *Rust v. Sullivan* (1991), he joined Chief Justice Rehnquist, and justices White, Scalia, and Kennedy in a ruling that prohibited any family planning project receiving federal funds from counseling or encouraging abortion as a method of family planning. Pro-choice advocates had claimed that these regulations violated the free-speech rights of doctors and other family planners, but to no avail. Tony Auth drew a cartoon for the *Philadelphia Inquirer* that sarcastically referred to the result as one of the "Great Moments in Medicine." With White looking on approvingly in the background, Souter is helping Scalia and Kennedy hold down a doctor while Rehnquist, who wrote the majority opinion in *Rust,* is stitching the doctor's mouth shut. The cartoon artfully captures the free-speech objection to the regulation that was rejected by the Court.

In 1991, when Bush nominated Clarence Thomas, a conservative black judge, to replace retiring Thurgood Marshall, the first African American to serve on the nation's high court and a prominent member of its liberal wing, the Senate Judiciary Committee asked the nominee many of the same questions it had leveled against Souter the year before. Liberal senators, such as Edward Kennedy and Howard Metzenbaum, arguably tried to kill Thomas's nomination by revealing his opposition to *Roe* and the constitutional right to an abortion. Gene Basset for the *Atlanta Journal* comments on the situation in a cartoon he drew during the confirmation hearings. Kennedy and Metzenbaum are dumping Thomas headfirst into the vat of *Roe v. Wade,* purportedly not to drown him, but to see if he passes "a liberal litmus test." The term "litmus test" had become popular among liberals during the 1980s to criticize the way Ronald Reagan had purportedly used tight pro-life criteria in his selection of Supreme Court nominees. Evidently, in Basset's opinion, liberals in the 1990s were hypocritically doing what they had condemned Reagan for doing in the past. In his confirmation hearing, when asked about his views on abortion, Thomas said he had never given much thought to the issue, a claim which some senators did not find very credible. Eventually the committee sent his nomination to the full Senate without a recommendation. Anita Hill's allegation that Thomas had sexually harassed her triggered more hearings, but the Senate ultimately confirmed Thomas by a vote of 52 to 48.

Following the Court's *Webster* decision, the battle over abortion shifted to the state legislatures. A re-energized pro-choice movement was able to defend a woman's right to an abortion in many states, but not in all. For example, Pennsylvania

" THIS IS NOT AN ATTEMPT TO DROWN JUDGE THOMAS... JUST A LIBERAL LITMUS TEST. "

AND THE BABY WILL BE HERE IN TIME FOR YOUR CONVENTION! ISN'T THAT WONDERFUL, DEAR?

added a twenty-four-hour waiting period for abortions, mandated spousal notification, and required all abortion clinics to inform women fully about the abortion procedure and what other alternatives were available. In 1992, a presidential election year, the Supreme Court reviewed the constitutionality of these provisions in *Planned Parenthood v. Casey*. Jeff Macnelly drew a cartoon for the *Chicago Tribune* that underscored the political implications of the upcoming Supreme Court decision. It depicts the Supreme Court as a judge pregnant with the "Penn abortion case." The judge informs a rattled Bush that the baby will be in time for his convention, adding "Isn't that wonderful, dear?" The term of endearment hints that Bush is responsible for the Court's condition, perhaps because he

supported the kind of regulations involved in the Pennsylvania case. He will therefore have to pay the political price in the upcoming election if the decision rallies the pro-choice movement against Bush and the Republican Party.

In the end, the Court's decision in *Casey* was very divided and complicated. Four justices (Rehnquist, White, Scalia, and Thomas) voted to uphold all the regulations and overrule *Roe;* two justices (Blackmun and Stevens) voted to invalidate all the regulations and preserve *Roe* in its entirety; and three justices (O'Connor, Kennedy, and Souter) voted to invalidate only the regulation requiring spousal notification. These three crucial swing justices preserved the "essential holding of *Roe*" but abandoned its trimester framework. Keeping *Roe*'s "central

core," they argued, was necessary to preserve the Court's legitimacy by not appearing to be under the political influence of the pro-life movement. The trimester framework should be replaced by an "undue burden" standard, they insisted, which would mean that states could regulate abortions during the pre-viability period as long as the regulations did not constitute "undue burdens" on a woman's right to have an abortion.

The Court's decision in *Casey* pleased neither side of the abortion controversy. Dick Wright drew a cartoon for the *Providence* (R.I.) *Journal-Bulletin* that echoed this reality. A father is reading the "Supreme Court Abortion Decision" to his two children, a pro-life Republican elephant and a pro-choice Democratic donkey. The story ends on the note, "They all lived unhappily ever after." In general, that has been the fate of the Supreme Court's role in the abortion controversy. Though the majority of the American people are more or less content with the Court's judicially imposed compromise, advocates on both sides of the debate are not satisfied with the status quo. ▣

Equal Rights
Amendment

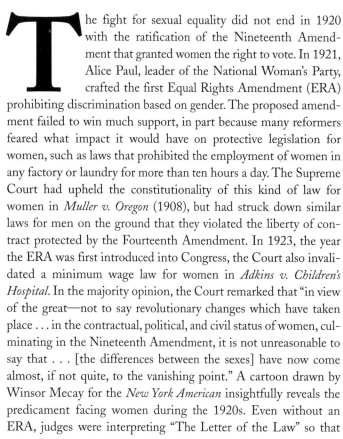

CHAPTER 16

Equal Rights Amendment

The fight for sexual equality did not end in 1920 with the ratification of the Nineteenth Amendment that granted women the right to vote. In 1921, Alice Paul, leader of the National Woman's Party, crafted the first Equal Rights Amendment (ERA) prohibiting discrimination based on gender. The proposed amendment failed to win much support, in part because many reformers feared what impact it would have on protective legislation for women, such as laws that prohibited the employment of women in any factory or laundry for more than ten hours a day. The Supreme Court had upheld the constitutionality of this kind of law for women in *Muller v. Oregon* (1908), but had struck down similar laws for men on the ground that they violated the liberty of contract protected by the Fourteenth Amendment. In 1923, the year the ERA was first introduced into Congress, the Court also invalidated a minimum wage law for women in *Adkins v. Children's Hospital.* In the majority opinion, the Court remarked that "in view of the great—not to say revolutionary changes which have taken place . . . in the contractual, political, and civil status of women, culminating in the Nineteenth Amendment, it is not unreasonable to say that . . . [the differences between the sexes] have now come almost, if not quite, to the vanishing point." A cartoon drawn by Winsor Mecay for the *New York American* insightfully reveals the predicament facing women during the 1920s. Even without an ERA, judges were interpreting "The Letter of the Law" so that

LAW VS. COMMON SENSE

HAPPY FATHERS DAY

women could not be favored over men. Given this background, it is not surprising that the ERA made little progress in the first half of the twentieth century.

Though the ERA was introduced into each session of Congress from 1923 onward, it was not until the resurgence of the women's rights movement during the 1960s that it had any realistic chance of passage. Finally, in March of 1972, under the urging of the National Organization for Women and ERAmerica, a coalition of dozens of organizations, Congress passed by the required two-thirds majority an amendment that read "Equality of rights under the law shall not be denied or abridged by the United States or by any state on account of sex." Since a number of states quickly ratified the ERA, proponents of the amendment were at first unconcerned about the seven-year deadline for ratification that Congress had incorporated into the proposal. Gene McCarty drew a cartoon commenting on the situation for San Bernadino, California's *Sun-Telegram*. It shows a middle-aged man vacuuming the carpet under his wife's feet as she reads a newspaper reporting that half of the thirty-eight states needed for the ERA's ratification have already "signed." The entertaining caption reads, "Happy Fathers Day," which fell on June 18 in 1972.

The pace of ratification, however, slowed significantly as opposition to the ERA coalesced under the leadership of Phyllis Schlafly, leader of the Eagle Forum/STOP ERA. By the end of 1972, twenty-two states had ratified the ERA, but there were only eight ratifications in 1973, three in 1974, one in 1975, and none in 1976. The arguments that opponents used to defeat the ERA varied from state to state, but one of the more common objections was that it would require drafting women into the military and placing them in combat roles. Eugene Craig published a cartoon on this theme in the *Columbus* (Ohio) *Dispatch*. It depicts an amazed Neptune staring at a female sailor dancing on the deck of an aircraft carrier. Under the caption "Mixed Reactions," a female figure symbolizing the wives of male sailors cautions, "Just a minute." The

Roots

impression left by the cartoon is that wives of men in the armed forces ought to think twice before they support the ERA.

During the 1970s, as the ERA came under increasing opposition, the Supreme Court decided a series of cases that gradually extended to women and men more constitutional protection against laws that discriminated on the basis of sex. In *Reed v. Reed* (1971), the Court invalidated a state law that preferred men to women as administrators of the estates of those dying without a will. In *Frontiero v. Richardson* (1973), it threw out a federal law that assumed that the wives of male members of the armed forces were dependent on them, while females had to prove the dependency of their husbands. And finally, in *Craig v. Boren* (1976), the Court struck down an Oklahoma law that permitted the sale of 3.2 percent beer to females over eighteen years of age but prohibited the sale to males under twenty-one years. In this line of cases, the Court fashioned a constitutional standard for laws that discriminated on the basis of gender that was somewhat lower than the standard applied to laws that discriminated on the basis of race or ethnicity. The latter kind of law had to have a "compelling purpose" and the use of a racial or an ethnic classification had to be a "necessary means" to that purpose. In contrast, laws that used sexual classifications had to be "substantially related" to "an important governmental pur-

pose." Though this latter standard was somewhat more relaxed than the former, the Court applied it forcefully, making it difficult for sexually discriminatory laws to pass constitutional muster, a result that tended to undermine the perceived need for the ERA.

In 1977, Indiana became the thirty-fifth state to ratify the ERA. Only three more states were needed to make the amendment a part of the Constitution. NOW sponsored an economic boycott of the fifteen states that so far had refused to ratify the amendment. Cities like Chicago, Las Vegas, and New Orleans lost millions of dollars of revenue from conventions, but the boycott had no discernible effect on the ERA's fate. A cartoon by Jack Bender published in the *Waterloo* (Iowa) *Courier* illuminates the plight of the ERA. It pictures the ERA as an aging woman runner coming to a standstill before the finish line, her legs transformed into tree roots. March 1979 was the seven-year deadline that Congress had placed in the proposed amendment in 1972. Bender, perhaps alluding to the popular novel by Alex Haley entitled *Roots,* is doubtful that the ERA will make it to the finish line.

Realizing that they would not be able to meet the March 1979 deadline, proponents of the ERA in 1978 sought an extension from Congress. Opponents objected that the extension was unconstitutional because the seven-year deadline was an integral part of the amendment. If the extension was granted, the states that had already ratified the ERA, they argued, would have to re-ratify it. Supporters knew that such a requirement would destroy any chance of the ERA's ratification. After all, four states had already rescinded their earlier votes in favor of the amendment. The con-stitutionalities of these rescissions were just as controversial as the extension. In the past, the Supreme Court had refused to decide the constitu-tionality of such issues, ruling in *Coleman v. Miller* (1939) that they were "political questions" subject to Congress's discretion.

While the debate over the constitutionality of the extension and the rescissions drained the political energy of the ERA movement, cartoonists visually articulated their contrasting points of view. A cartoon by Etta Hulme that appeared in the *Fort Worth Star-Telegram* characterized the ERA as a forlorn prisoner chained to a wall in a dungeon. Her two male jailors refuse to deal her into their card game on the ground that it would require changing the rules in the mid-dle of a game of "discriminatory laws." Refusing to grant an extension for the ERA, in Hulme's opinion, would seem to be just another case of men refusing to give up the benefits they receive from a system of sexual inequality. In contrast, Ed Gamble drew a car-toon for the *Nashville Banner* that ridiculed the extension. It would be like extending a prizefight beyond the normal fifteen rounds. In the cartoon, the ERA is symbolized as a badly beaten female boxer. One of her corner men—the Justice Department— informs her that the fight will go on until she wins. The dazed look on the ERA's face suggests that Gamble might be predicting that the ERA, even with an extension, would not be ratified.

Following a large ERA demonstration in Wash-ington on July 9, Congress granted the extension in

"DEAL YOU IN ? YOU EXPECT US TO CHANGE RULES IN THE MIDDLE OF THE GAME ?"

"GOOD NEWS... WE'VE DECIDED TO EXTEND THE FIGHT UNTIL YOU WIN!"

All Is Forgiven?

SOMETHING'S WRONG... WHAT'S WRONG?

AN EMERGENCY TENANTS' MEETING HAS BEEN CALLED AT THE BOARDING HOUSE.

THIS JUNE 20TH, THE SUPREME COURT RULED THAT "MALE-ONLY" CLUBS ARE UNCONSTITUTIONAL...

WELL NOTHING'S MORE "MALE ONLY" THAN BLOOM COUNTY! WE'VE GOT TO INTRODUCE A WOMAN!!

WE'RE SO SORRY.

WHAT'S NEXT? UNISEX UNDERWEAR? PHYLLIS SCHLAFLY WAS RIGHT!

August of 1978. The new deadline for ratification was June 30, 1982. Since Congress had taken the position that the rescissions were invalid, the ERA would be ratified if three of the fifteen remaining states would approve it. Surprisingly, despite heavy lobbying by the ERA forces, state after state refused to ratify the amendment, some of them voting down the measure time and time again. In 1980, President Jimmy Carter, an ERA supporter, proposed registering women for the military draft, which caused an immediate backlash against the ERA. At its 1980 convention, the Republican Party voted down an ERA plank that had been a part of its platform for forty years. Throughout the 1980 presidential race, Republican nominee Ronald Reagan opposed the ERA, but pledged to appoint a woman to the Supreme Court. In the first year of his administration, President Reagan kept his promise by appointing Sandra Day O'Connor to the seat vacated by Justice Potter Stewart. A cartoon by Jim Lange that appeared in *The Daily Oklahoman* reflects how women reacted to O'Connor's appointment to the high court. A spinsterish-looking woman cries in joy at receiving a bouquet of flowers from the White House

florist. However, the question mark following the caption "All is forgiven" is a hint that some women would never forgive Reagan for his opposition to the ERA.

Though it upheld a statutory rape law that only punished men in *Michael M. v Superior Court* (1981) and a draft registration law that only required males to register for the draft in *Rostker v. Goldberg* (1981), the Supreme Court ruled that a state could not have an all-female nursing school in *Mississippi University for Women v. Hogan* in 1982—the same year the ERA died because the deadline for its ratification passed. In 1983, a new ERA was introduced into the House of Representatives, but it failed to pass. The following year the Supreme Court held that the Jaycees, a traditionally male-only organization, could be found guilty of discrimination if women were excluded from membership. After the Court handed down a similar ruling outlawing male-only clubs in *New York State Club Association v. New York City* (1988), Berke Breathed drew a cartoon facetiously claiming that these decisions meant that a woman would have to be introduced into his popular cartoon strip Bloom County. "What's next? Unisex underwear?" the playful penguin asks and concludes that Phyllis Schlafly, the woman who led the fight against the ERA, "was right!"

In 1994, the Supreme Court arguably made sexual discrimination even more difficult to justify by ruling that lawyers could not use their preemptory challenges to exclude women or men from juries on the basis of their sex. Such challenges reinforce impermissible gender stereotypes, the Court argued, and do not have the kind of "exceedingly persuasive justification" needed to justify sexual classifications. Two years later, the Court ruled that Virginia could no longer operate the Virginia Military Institute as a male-only military school. VMI, established in 1839, had to admit women even if this meant that the school had to change its harsh "adversative method" of training and education. Chuck Asay drew a cartoon for the *Colorado Springs Gazette Telegraph* that denigrated the Court's action. Under the caption "Change of Command," it shows the military handing the American flag over to Justice Ruth Bader Ginsburg, the second woman appointed to the Supreme Court and the author of the majority opinion in the VMI case, while female "social engineers" holding the Court's ruling look on approvingly. It could be said that Asay's cartoon is misleading because only a minority of recent graduates of VMI have pursued military careers, but it's also true that relatively few women have matriculated at VMI since the 1996 decision. In any case, decisions such as these by the Supreme Court have continued to erode support for the ERA. Though proposals for a new ERA have been introduced into each session of Congress since the deadline for the old ERA expired in 1982, neither house has taken any action on them. ⚖

Affirmative Action

CHAPTER 17

Affirmative Action

In 1965, President Lyndon Johnson issued Executive Order 11246, which directed all companies having contracts with the federal government to use "affirmative action" in their hiring and promotion decisions. From this somewhat humble origin, the practice of giving members of minority groups preferences in the fields of public contracts, employment, and education became increasingly widespread. In a speech at Howard University, Johnson justified affirmative action by referring to the metaphor of a race. He said that if a person who had been "hobbled by chains" for years was unshackled, he or she could not be expected to compete successfully against those who had been free to train for the race. Simple fairness required that a "head start" be given to such an individual. In the same way, Johnson intimated, African Americans and other minorities who have suffered from discrimination in the past should today receive preferences from government, private employers, and educational institutions. Justified on these grounds, affirmative action spread widely throughout the late 1960s and early 1970s. The liberal spirit animating these efforts to remedy the effects of past discrimination reverberates in a cartoon drawn by Tom Engelhardt published in the *St. Louis Post-Dispatch* on October 13, 1977. It shows a white man reaching down to help a black man over a wall. The caption reads, "After holding 'em down for so long, why not a little helping up?"

The Supreme Court considered the constitutionality of affirmative action for the first time in the landmark decision of *Regents of*

'After Holding 'Em Down For So Long, Why Not
A Little Helping Up?'

University of California v. Bakke (1978). The case involved the medical school of the University of California at Davis. Each year it set aside sixteen of one hundred spaces for minority students. Even though Allan Bakke's test scores and grades were higher than many of the minority students who had been admitted, the school twice denied him admission. Frustrated, Bakke filed suit, claiming that the medical school was discriminating against him on the basis of his race. The Supreme Court split evenly on the issue. Four justices ruled that Davis's affirmative action plan was unlawful, while four others insisted that it was not. Justice Lewis Powell, the deciding vote, agreed with the first four justices that Davis's plan, because of its quota-like character, was illegal. A public school could not reserve sixteen spaces exclusively for minority applicants. However, Powell continued, for the sake of obtaining a diverse student body, a school could use race as a "plus" in deciding whether to admit individual students. In short, the medical school had treated Bakke unlawfully, but it could still practice a form of affirmative action. A cartoon drawn by Tom Curtis for the *Milwaukee Sentinel* characterizes the Court's *Bakke* decision as a two-faced judge looking in opposite directions.

Despite the Court's splintered decision in *Bakke*, leaders in education, business, and government relied heavily on Justice Powell's pivotal opinion to establish affirmative-action programs that avoided the appearance of quotas. Supporting this trend, the Court ruled in *United Steelworkers v. Weber* (1979) that private employers could voluntarily eliminate racial imbalances in job categories by using race-conscious hiring goals and in *Fullilove v. Klutznick* (1980) that the federal government could seek to remedy the effects of past discrimination by requiring that ten percent of federal funds granted for local public works projects go to minority-owned

Affirmative inaction

OLD BOY NETWORK

COURT LIMITS MINORITY SET-ASIDES

DISCRIMINA-TION MUST BE PROVED

JOE DOES ROOFING $$

need a plumber? call Al

NEED A LAWYER? CALL DAN

"I'VE NEVER DISCRIMINATED AGAINST A MINORITY. I DON'T EVEN KNOW ONE."

businesses. The quota-like character of the latter program was not fatal because, based on the Fourteenth Amendment, the federal government had a special responsibility and power to remedy racial discrimination. Affirmative action therefore flourished throughout much of the 1980s, though opposition to it continued to mount.

In 1989 the Court changed course. In *Richmond v. J. A. Croson Co.,* a 6 to 3 decision, it denied Richmond, Virginia, the power it had earlier granted to the federal government in *Fullilove*. Before Richmond could set aside a percentage of its construction contracts for minority businesses, it had to prove that the city or its prime contractors had, in fact, discriminated against minorities in the past. It could not base its affirmative action policy on the fact that minorities were victims of "societal discrimination." A cartoon by Tony Auth that appeared in the *Philadelphia Inquirer*

on January 25, 1989, questions whether the Court's decision in *Croson* is at all realistic or defensible. Two old white gentlemen of the "Old Boy Network" are relaxing by a fire at their club. After reading how the Court has limited minority set-asides, one says to the other, "I've never discriminated against a minority. I don't even know one." Auth's point is that racial discrimination is often societal in character. A white contractor who doesn't even know a member of a minority group is arguably engaging in a subtle but pernicious form of discrimination, but the Court's *Croson* ruling meant that the effects of such discrimination would go unremedied.

Mirroring the divisions within American society, the Supreme Court during the 1990s remained deeply divided about the constitutionality of affirmative action. In *Metro Broadcasting Co. v. Federal Communications Commission* (1990), a 5 to 4 decision, it

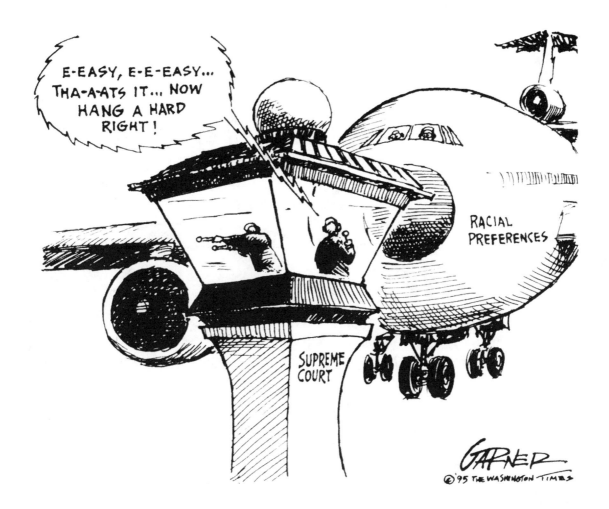

E-EASY, E-E-EASY... THA-A-ATS IT... NOW HANG A HARD RIGHT!

RACIAL PREFERENCES

SUPREME COURT

GARNER

© '95 THE WASHINGTON TIMES

upheld federal policies that made it easier for minority members to acquire broadcasting stations. Five years later, however, after a turnover of three justices, the Court reversed course. In *Adarand Constructors Inc. v. Pena*, a 6 to 3 decision, the Court overturned *Metro Broadcasting Co.* and ruled that federal affirmative action programs must satisfy the so-called "strict scrutiny" test, which would require that the program in question be a "necessary" means to a "compelling" purpose. Given the way the Court had applied this test in other contexts, it was

arguable that affirmative action programs would be more difficult to justify after *Adarand* than before.

Cartoonists reacted to *Adarand* in diverse ways. Bill Garner drew a cartoon for the *Washington Times* that seems to support the decision. It pictures a large airliner, symbolizing "racial preferences," about to crash into the control tower of the Supreme Court. To prevent the disaster, the traffic controller advises the pilot to "hang a hard right!" On the one hand, Garner's cartoon hints that the Court has saved itself by directing the plane to

the political right; on the other, by turning right and landing the plane under the Supreme Court's guidance, "racial preferences" will fly no more.

A cartoon drawn by Walt Handelsman expresses the opposite point of view. One "redneck" sitting on a porch says to another, "Purty doggone sensible for six college boys, two little ladies, and a colored fella." The newspaper that the "redneck" is reading confirms that he's talking about the Supreme Court. The headlines report that "private white clubs can ban blacks" and that the Court has okayed excluding gays, a clear reference to *Hurley v. Irish-American Gay, Lesbian, and Bisexual Group of Boston* (1995), a case in which the Supreme Court ruled that

the organizers of Boston's St. Patrick's Day Parade could exclude gay and lesbian groups from the event. The last headline describes what the Court did in *Adarand*: "The Supreme Court rolls back affirmative action." While Garner's cartoon seemingly endorses what the Court did in *Adarand*, Handelsman's, it would appear, is suggesting that the decision is "sensible" only in the eyes of bigots and homophobes.

In 1996, the required four justices did not vote to place an affirmative action case from the Fifth Circuit—*Texas v. Hopwood*—on the Supreme Court's docket. Refusing to abide by Justice Powell's opinion in *Bakke*, the lower court had struck down the University of Texas Law School's affirmative action plan, thereby making it illegal for any public school to use race as a factor in admissions within the boundaries of the Fifth Circuit—an area comprising Texas, Louisiana, and Mississippi. Powell's *Bakke* opinion on affirmative action was not controlling, the lower court insisted, because it had never garnered the support of a majority of the justices and because recent Supreme Court decisions made it clear that student diversity was not the sort of compelling state interest that was required for an affirmative action plan to pass strict scrutiny. Some commentators have sharply criticized the Court's decision not to review *Hopwood*, arguing that the Court was ducking an important constitutional issue, while others have endorsed it, arguing that it would be unwise for the Court to preempt the democratic process. A cartoon drawn by Joseph Azah and published in *Legal Times* on July 8, 1996, can be understood as a figurative comment on the Court's dilemma. It pictures the justices warily eyeing a skunk sitting on the steps of the Supreme Court. The skunk symbolizes affirmative action because Azah's cartoon is adjacent to an article by Stuart Taylor Jr. entitled "Ducking *Hopwood*: The Passive Virtues." Though the cartoon is clearly implying that the Court is keeping its distance from affirmative action, it does not say whether this reluctance is unjustifiable fear or healthy prudence.

Also in 1996, the voters of California approved Proposition 209, an amendment to the state constitution that prohibited the state from using racial preferences in public education, employment, and contracting. Almost immediately, Thelton Henderson, a federal district judge, suspended the implementation of Proposition 209 on the ground that such legally mandated equality of opportunity would violate the Equal Protection Clause. The judge's ruling seemed to treat affirmative action not as a controversial policy that states could, if they wished, use in clearly defined circumstances, but rather as a mandatory policy that states must pursue. The paradox of requiring permanent racial preferences on the ground of equality was humorously parodied by Dick Wright in a cartoon that appeared in the *Columbus* (Ohio) *Dispatch* in December of 1996. It shows a judge absurdly insisting on such preferences because the use of racial preferences constitutes discrimination that must in turn be remedied by the use of more racial preferences. The Ninth Circuit Court of Appeals reversed Henderson's decision and opposition to affirmative action continues to exist across the country.

Notwithstanding this American ambivalence about racial preferences, the Supreme Court gave affirmative action a big boost in *Grutter v. Bollinger* (2003). Relying heavily on Justice Powell's *Bakke* opinion, a five-justice majority upheld the use of race as a plus in law school admissions for the purpose of obtaining the educational benefits that flow from a diverse student body. The Court indicated, however, that affirmative action would no longer be permissible in higher education if and when these benefits could be achieved by race-neutral means, which, in the Court's view, was likely to happen within a twenty-five-year period. Accordingly, though the decision favored affirmative action, it also suggested that what had been intended as a "helping hand" would not be allowed to become a permanent crutch. ⚖

Free Press

...MURDER, RAPE AND ROBBERY... HOW 'BOUT YOU?
INVESTIGATIVE REPORTING...

CHAPTER 18

Free Press

The First Amendment proclaims that "Congress shall make no law . . . abridging the freedom of speech, *or of the press*." It could be argued that the Constitution's separate reference to the "freedom of the press" should be the basis for granting newspaper reporters rights and privileges in addition to those protected by the freedom-of-speech clause. For example, perhaps a reporter should have more of a constitutional right than the average citizen to refuse to comply with governmental demands for information. On the other hand, who qualifies as a member of the "press"? Presumably a reporter working for a major newspaper would, but what of a reporter for a college newspaper? A high school newspaper? A freelance writer for a magazine? An author? A pamphleteer? A disgruntled advocate who maintains a website? Confronting these kinds of issues in two controversial cases during the 1970s, a sharply divided Court decided not to grant the press any special rights based on the freedom-of-press clause. In part because they are natural allies of the press, cartoonists attacked the Court's position vehemently.

In the early 1970s, Paul Branzburg, a reporter for the *Louisville (Ky.) Courier-Journal,* Paul Pappas, a television reporter for a Massachusetts television station, and Earl Caldwell, a reporter for the *New York Times,* each received a subpoena to testify before a grand jury about information they had gained in their professional capacity as members of the press. Branzburg had written two stories on

'I'm Aiming at the Apple'

the manufacture and sale of illicit drugs in Kentucky; Pappas and Caldwell had firsthand knowledge of the possibly unlawful activities of the Black Panther party. The three reporters fought the subpoenas, claiming that they had a right, based on freedom of the press, to keep their sources confidential. In *Branzburg v. Hayes* (1972), the Supreme Court ruled 5 to 4 against the reporters. In his majority opinion, Justice Byron White insisted that reporters had a duty, just like any other citizen, to answer grand jury questions. In his opinion, a privilege to keep sources confidential was neither necessary nor wise. Even if no privilege is recognized, the vast majority of sources would continue to talk to reporters because they were not criminals or witnesses of crime. And even if a few criminals or witnesses of crime were discouraged from talking to the press, White concluded, it was more important to prosecute crime in courtrooms than read about crime in newspapers.

In his dissenting opinion, Justice Potter Stewart argued that the Court's decision would erode the independence of the press by transforming it into an investigative arm of the state. The press would routinely gather information that the state would then use to convict individuals. Such a system would inevitably have a negative impact on the "broad societal interest in a full and free flow of information to the public." Accordingly, Stewart concluded, a right to publish implies a right to gather the news, which in turn implies "a right to a confidential relationship between a reporter and his source." The right, however, was not absolute. Despite the privilege, a reporter must answer a grand jury's questions if the government can 1) show probable cause that the reporter has information of a specific violation of the law; 2) demonstrate that the information cannot be obtained by any "alternative means less destructive of First Amendment rights"; and 3) reveal a compelling and overriding interest in the information.

"ONE MORE TIME—ARE YOU READY TO REVEAL YOUR NEWS SOURCES?"

Cartoonists portrayed the *Branzburg* decision as an assault on the basic principle of a free press. A cartoon drawn by Don Hesse for the *St. Louis Globe-Democrat* was one such example. Those who demand "news source disclosure" claim they are aiming at the apple of criminal evidence on the head of "press freedom," but in fact they are aiming at the free press's very heart. In contrast, a cartoon drawn by Pat Oliphant for the *Los Angeles Times* Syndicate uses the image of a chopping block. Because he refuses to reveal his sources to the courts, a reporter whose head is draped over a typewriter is about to be decapitated by a blindfolded Lady Justice. The verbal exchange in the lower left-hand corner alludes to the fact that several reporters were imprisoned after they were found in contempt of court for refusing to disclose sources at the same time that it suggests that the Court *Branzburg* decision was contemptible. Both of these cartoons reflect the press's extreme dissatisfaction with the Court's ruling.

Many lower courts have been reluctant to follow the harsh rule enunciated in Justice White's majority opinion in *Branzburg*,

preferring instead not to force reporters to disclose their sources except in exceptional circumstances where the needs of law enforcement are paramount. Moreover, during the 1970s over half the state legislatures passed so-called "shield laws" that gave reporters limited immunity from grand jury testimony. A cartoon drawn by Bill Sanders for the Publishers-Hall Syndicate comments on this trend by asking why these shield laws are needed. They are required, the cartoon indicates, because the press and the First Amendment were stabbed in the back by the "Burger Supreme Court." These shield laws give reporters a qualified privilege not to disclose their sources, but it's not the absolute constitutional privilege that reporters wanted in 1972.

Six years after *Branzburg*, in *Zurcher v. Stanford Daily*, the Supreme Court considered whether a judge could issue an *ex parte* search warrant authorizing a police search of a campus newspaper office for photographs of a violent demonstration. The campus newspaper claimed that the issuance of a search warrant, rather than a subpoena for the photographs in ques-

"What do you need a shield law for?"

tion, violated the freedom of the press protected by the First Amendment. In a majority opinion again written by Justice White, the Court ruled against the newspaper, holding that the search warrant violated neither the Fourth Amendment's protection against unreasonable searches and seizures nor the First Amendment's guarantee of a free press. Tom Engelhardt drew a cartoon for the *St. Louis Post-Dispatch* that denounced the Court's ruling. Over the caption, "Hey, we're getting better!," the Court has just killed two birds with the single stone of the "newspaper office search decision." Unfortunately, the two birds are "American eagles": the First and Fourth amendments.

In response to the same decision, Etta Hulme drew a piquant cartoon for the *Fort Worth Star-Telegram*. It shows an editor, holding a report of the Court's "newspaper search" decision, asking one of the justices of the Supreme Court for a search warrant to search the Supreme Court's courtroom for the First Amendment. "We suspect it's tucked away around here somewhere," the editor exclaims.

Justice Stewart wrote a strong dissent in *Zurcher*, arguing that search warrants of newspaper offices should not be issued unless there was probable cause to believe that the evidence could not be obtained by a subpoena. Subpoenas, in his opinion, were preferable because they would allow the press to make a motion to quash the subpoena, which would in turn require an adversarial hearing in front of a judge before the press would have to hand over the subpoenaed material. In contrast, the press could challenge *ex parte* warrants only after the police had searched a newsroom, that is, only after the constitutional damage had been done. Because of these kinds of concerns, Congress enacted the Privacy Protection Act in 1980, which required state and federal law enforcement to seek a subpoena to obtain documents from anyone engaged

'Hey, We're Getting Better!'

ETTA HULME FORT WORTH STAR-TELEGRAM N.E.A. '78

"WELL, THEN HOW ABOUT ISSUING US A WARRANT TO SEARCH THESE PREMISES FOR THE FIRST AMENDMENT—WE SUSPECT IT'S TUCKED AWAY AROUND HERE SOMEWHERE"

Ah, But I'm Not The Congress

U.S. NEWSPAPER REPORTER

U.S. CONSTITUTION 1ST AMENDMENT: "THE CONGRESS SHALL MAKE NO LAW... ABRIDGING THE FREEDOM OF... THE PRESS..."

THE COURTS

Reg-Manning
Republic editorial cartoonist

in "the communications industry." A judge could issue a search warrant only if there was a reasonable fear that the documents would be destroyed.

Actions by state legislatures and Congress have to some extent circumvented the Supreme Court decisions of the 1970s. Today reporters have more immunity from search warrants and grand jury subpoenas than average citizens. These protections, however, rest on statute, not the Constitution, and they are not absolute. This became abundantly clear in 1979 when Myron Farber, a reporter for the *New York Times,* wrote a series of articles suggesting that a mysterious "Dr. X" was responsible for a number of deaths in a New Jersey hospital. The resulting police investigation led to the indictment of Dr. Mario Jascalevich, who was accused of murdering five people by injecting them with curare, a muscle relaxant. During the trial, the defense asked the trial court to order Farber to turn over all his notes and papers pertaining to Dr. X and the murders. Despite the existence of a New Jersey shield law, the trial judge granted the defense's request on the ground that defendants have a Sixth Amendment right to exculpatory evidence, but Farber and the *New York Times* refused to hand over the materials. Finding both the reporter and the newspaper in contempt of court, the trial judge jailed Farber and fined the *New York Times* $100,000 plus an additional $5,000 a day until it complied with the court's order.

Cartoonists around the country rallied to Farber's defense. Reg Manning drew a cartoon for the *Arizona Republic* that shows Farber behind bars confronting a judge with the free press clause of the First Amendment. The judge cavalierly dismisses the significance of the language with the observation that a literal reading supports the conclusion that it only prohibits what Congress can do, not the courts. The Supreme Court has, in fact, never

THE BURGER COURT

sanctioned such an extreme position. Though a judge's discretion to find individuals in contempt of court for disobeying a court order is considerable, it is not absolute. Judges as well as presidents have to respect the principles enshrined therein.

The *Palm Beach Post* published a cartoon by S. C. Rawls that highlighted the disparity between Farber's "crime" and his punishment. Even though Farber was only "guilty" of investigative reporting, he was being punished like someone who had committed murder, rape, and robbery. The tone of the cartoon is playful, but its message is not completely farfetched. In cases of civil contempt, the purpose of imprisonment is not to punish reporters but to convince them to comply with the court's order. As long as they refuse to disclose their sources, a judge theoretically can keep them imprisoned indefinitely.

When the case came before it, the New Jersey Supreme Court released Farber and suspended the fines against the *New York Times*, but this relief was only temporary. On October 11, 1980, the state high court reinstated the trial judge's ruling. Even with New Jersey's shield law, Dr. Jascalevich's constitutional right to obtain evidence in his defense outweighed a reporter's right not to disclose confidential sources. Back in jail, Farber did not give up. He and the *Times* appealed to the United States Supreme Court, but to no avail. Their case was unable to garner the four votes needed to place it on the Court's docket. Jim Borgman of the *Cincinnati Enquirer* drew a brilliant cartoon that mocked the Court's timidity. The nine justices are standing in the background staring down at a newspaperman holding the bars of his cell, which Borgman artfully identifies with the white spaces between the justices' robes. The insinuation is that the Supreme Court was responsible for Farber's incarceration even though the justices did not accept the case for review.

As Farber and the *New York Times* pursued their appeals, the murder trial of Dr. Jascalevich proceeded onward without the evidence the defense was demanding. Soon after Farber was jailed for the second time and the Supreme Court refused to hear his case, the jury returned a verdict of not guilty. Since the trial was over, Farber's imprisonment and the fines came to an end. The total amount of fines assessed against the *New York Times* was $285,000, though eventually the New Jersey courts refunded most of the money. Of course, no one could give back to Myron Farber the days he spent in prison. His experience defending his professional convictions places into sharp relief the implications of the Supreme Court's decisions denying the press any special constitutional right to resist governmental demands for information. Legislatures can grant the press special immunities from grand jury subpoenas or special protections from search warrants. However, when a defendant's right to obtain evidence comes into conflict with a reporter's right not to disclose sources, the Court has ruled that the latter must give way because the former is constitutionally rooted while the latter is not. ⚖

CHAPTER 19

Flag Burning

In *Texas v. Johnson* (1989), the Supreme Court ruled that burning the American flag was protected by the free speech clause of the First Amendment. The decision was a sharp departure from earlier law. Flag desecration had been punished for decades, though the penalties for such acts of defiance were usually no more than a small fine and/or a month in jail. During the Civil War, however, Union General Benjamin Butler ordered the execution of William B. Mumford after he was convicted of treason in New Orleans by a military court for dragging the Stars and Stripes through the mud and shredding it. Similarly, a Montana court during World War I harshly sentenced E. V. Starr to ten to twenty years at hard labor because he refused to kiss the flag and referred to it as "nothing but a piece of cotton." Though the Supreme Court in 1907 upheld the constitutionality of flag desecration statutes in *Halter v. Nebraska*, it ruled that states could not punish those who displayed red flags (a communist symbol) in *Stromberg v. California* (1931) or compel school children to salute the American flag in *West Virginia Board of Education v. Barnette* (1943). Not until 1969 did the Supreme Court in *Street v. New York* throw out laws punishing verbal disrespect of the flag. Five years later, in *Spence v. Washington*, the Court overturned the conviction of a man who taped a peace symbol to a flag on the ground that he had not permanently destroyed or disfigured it. These later decisions narrowed the ways in which states could protect the flag as a national symbol, yet they did not bar states

from punishing those who expressed their disrespect for the flag by physically destroying it, whether by fire or some other means.

Flag burning was relatively uncommon until protestors burned a flag at a massive anti-Vietnam War demonstration in New York City's Central Park on April 15, 1967. The American public reacted negatively to this widely publicized event and Congress quickly enacted a federal law prohibiting flag desecration. In response, the number of flag burnings rose dramatically. In 1973, the *Christian Science Monitor* estimated that a thousand flag-desecration cases had been prosecuted. Though many of these prosecutions were for less serious forms of flag desecration, a significant percentage were for burning the flag, which could easily end in a jail sentence for anyone convicted. It is therefore interesting, and somewhat ironic, that the Supreme Court did not hand down its major flag-burning decision until the end of the 1980s, a decade very different from that of the 1960s. Ronald Reagan, a conservative Republican, was president from 1981–1989, the economy was stable throughout most of the decade, and the country was at peace. Art Wood drew a cartoon contrasting the flag-burning days of the sixties to the flag-saluting days of the eighties. The cartoon underscores the fact that the Court handed down its groundbreaking decision on flag burning at a time when desecration was virtually non-existent.

The event that led to the Supreme Court's flag-burning decision took place on August 22, 1984. In front of the Dallas city hall, a small group of protestors objecting to the Republican Convention's re-nomination of Ronald Reagan as president formed a circle and burned a flag. Convicted of violating Texas's flag desecration statute, Gregory Lee Johnson appealed to the Supreme Court. On June 11, 1989, in a 5 to 4 decision, the Court ruled that Johnson's conduct in burning the flag was expressive political

AMERICAN PUBLIC OPINION:

A — TRAITOROUS RADICAL PUNK WHO OUGHT TO BE THROWN IN JAIL OR SHOT

B — HEROIC, PATRIOTIC STUDENT-REFORMER BRUTALLY JAILED OR SHOT FOR EXPRESSING BELIEFS

speech and therefore within the First Amendment. Texas had no interest in preventing flag burning that outweighed Johnson's right of free speech. The state's interest in maintaining order was not relevant because Johnson's act of burning the flag had neither caused nor threatened to cause any disturbance. And, though Texas may have an interest in preserving the flag as a national symbol, the free speech clause forbade government from using its coercive power against those who burn the flag to attack the values it symbolizes. "If we were to hold that a State may forbid flag burning wherever it is likely to endanger the flag's symbolic role, but allow it wherever burning a flag promotes that role—as where, for example, a person ceremoniously burns a dirty flag—we would be saying that when it comes to impairing the flag's physical integrity, the flag itself may be used as a symbol . . . in only one direction." A cartoon by Chris Obrion published in the *Potomac* (Va.) *News* indirectly illustrates the majority's reasoning. It shows an American and a

Chinese radical burning their respective countries' flags. In reacting to such incidents, American public opinion is fundamentally inconsistent. It condemns or applauds an expressive act depending on the speaker's ideology. In the same way, the Court implied, if government were to punish one kind of flag burning and not another, it would be engaging in censorship in violation of freedom of speech.

Many of the cartoons that appeared echoed the American public's generally negative reaction to the Court's *Johnson* decision. One by Hank McClure published in the *Lawton* (Texas) *Constitution* pictures a group of Vietnam veterans engaging in their own form of expressive conduct. Instead of burning a flag, they're burning the Supreme Court at the stake. The cartoon captures the elastic quality of the Court's concept of expressive conduct. If burning a flag is constitutionally protected, even though it doesn't involve either speech or writing, then what other types of actions can gain similar protection? Jim Dobbins,

SIGN OF THE TIMES

SUPREME COURT

MY STARS!

drawing for the *Union* (N.H.) *Leader,* takes a different tack by suggesting that the Court's decision is itself a form of flag desecration. His cartoon depicts the Supreme Court as a pontificating figure making a pronouncement with a flag patch on his rump. The placement of the patch is reminiscent of how many opponents of the Vietnam War expressed themselves during the 1960s and early 1970s. A cartoon drawn by John Shevchik for the *Valley* (Pa.) *Tribune* focuses on the irony of flag burners taking shelter behind the very values symbolized by the flag. It shows a tearful Uncle Sam unable to reconcile the fact that "Old Glory symbolizes [a] wide range of freedoms," including freedom of speech, with the Court's ruling that burning the flag is free speech.

Within a few weeks of the decision, both the Senate and the House of Representatives passed resolutions expressing disap-

pointment with the Court's ruling. On June 30, in a speech he delivered at the Iwo Jima Memorial in Arlington, Virginia, Republican President George Bush sponsored a constitutional amendment that would overturn *Johnson* and allow both Congress and the states to punish the physical desecration of the flag. A cartoon drawn by Pete Wagner characterizes Bush's proposed constitutional amendment as a hypocritical political maneuver. In the cartoon, Bush expresses outrage that anyone would use the flag for "cheap ideological theatrics," but the irony is that Bush himself was arguably guilty of "wrapping himself in the flag." During his victorious presidential campaign against Democrat Michael Dukakis in 1988, Bush repeatedly criticized the former governor of Massachusetts for vetoing a state law in 1977 that would have required public school teachers to lead students in reciting the Pledge of

Allegiance. To underscore his criticism of Dukakis, Bush visited flag factories, led audiences in reciting the pledge, and decked his campaign stops with numerous flags. The fact that in the cartoon Bush begins to recite the pledge after denouncing flag burning makes it relatively clear that Wagner is explicitly referring to Bush's use of the flag for his own political and ideological benefit during the 1988 campaign.

Rather than support Bush's option of a constitutional amendment, Democrats proposed enacting a new law. Their argument was that an amendment was unnecessary because a "content neutral" flag desecration statute—one that prohibited physically damaging the flag for any reason—would yet be constitutional because it would not be related to expression in any way. With the exception of worn flags, which were exempted by the statute on the ground that they were no longer "flags," no one could burn a flag, whether to express disrespect and contempt or honor and loyalty. A constitutional amendment should be pursued, the same Democrats argued, only as a last resort. Such "tinkering" with the Constitution was dangerous because it risked eroding the Bill of Rights by excessively amending it. Chuck Ayers drew a cartoon for the *Akron* (Ohio) *Beacon-Journal* that figuratively illuminated this particular argument. It shows one amendment after the other pasted onto the Bill of Rights, ending with one ("No Anti-Government Thoughts") that turned the flag upside down and stood the Constitution on its head.

The argument against "tinkering with the Constitution" eventually won the day and the Flag Protection Act became law on October 28, 1989, nine days after the Senate had refused to give Bush's constitutional amendment the necessary two-thirds approval. A cartoon by Jeff Stahler published in 1990 by the *Cincinnati Post* criticizes the new law

by alluding to a controversial art exhibit in Chicago the year before. At this exhibit, patrons were forced to walk on the flag if they wanted to write in a ledger how they felt the American flag should be displayed. In Stahler's cartoon, a figure symbolizing Congress walks on the Constitution with muddy shoes so that he can pledge allegiance to the flag.

Protestors across the country defied the Flag Protection Act as soon as it took effect on October 28, 1989. In response, the Justice Department prosecuted three individuals who burned several flags on the steps of the Capitol in Washington, D.C., on October 30. The district judge threw out the case on the ground that the act was unconstitutional, but the government appealed. Since the Flag Protection Act mandated expedited appellate review, the case quickly came before the Supreme Court. On June 11, 1990, the Court ruled against the federal government in *United States v. Eichman.* The same five justices who had formed the majority in *Johnson* rejected the government's contention that a content-neutral flag desecration law was constitutional. Even if the law neutrally prohibited all forms of physical desecration of the flag, no one could deny that the purpose of the law was to protect the flag's symbolic value. That in itself was sufficient to invalidate the law because it meant that the law's purpose was related to the suppression of expression. In other words, punishing those who burned the flag to show their respect for it did not change the underlying fact that the law's purpose was to punish those who burnt the flag to show their contempt for it. For that reason, the majority reasoned, the law was a violation of freedom of speech.

The Court's decision in *Eichman* meant that a constitutional amendment was the only way to stop flag burning as a means of political protest. However, such an amendment would for the first time in the nation's history carve out an explicit

FIGHTING FIRE WITH FIRE

exception to one of the fundamental guarantees of the Bill of Rights. A cartoon drawn by Chris Curtis for the *Potomac* (Md.) *Almanac* insightfully reveals the dilemma. Over the caption of "Fighting Fire With Fire," a young radical burns the flag while an older gentleman burns the First Amendment. In response to *Eichman* and the dilemma it posed, President Bush again called for a constitutional amendment, but his appeal failed to rouse the degree of public support that it had the year before. In late June, Bush's proposed amendment fell well short of the two-thirds majority required in both houses of Congress. Following this crucial vote, the number of incidents of flag burning waned.

After the elections of 1994, Republican Party majorities in both houses of Congress nonetheless proposed a constitutional amendment prohibiting flag burning that almost secured the number of votes needed to submit the measure to the states, falling just three votes short of Senate approval after having obtained the required two-thirds majority in the House. In 1997 and again in 1999, the process repeated itself, with the House passing a constitutional amendment prohibiting flag desecration and the Senate declining to do so. The stalemate is yet another indication of the divisive character of the constitutionality of punishing flag burning. ⚖

CHAPTER 20

The Clinton Impeachment Controversy

The Constitution grants Congress the power to remove a president from office if he has committed "treason, bribery, or other high crimes and misdemeanors." To exercise this power, the House of Representatives must first "impeach" (or charge) the president with an impeachable offense and then the Senate must, by a two-thirds vote, convict him at a trial. Throughout American history, only three presidents have faced the threat of impeachment. In 1868, Andrew Johnson was impeached for attempting to dismiss Secretary of War Edwin Stanton, in violation of a law that Congress had passed over his veto. Johnson escaped conviction and removal by one vote in the Senate. In 1974, the House Judiciary Committee adopted three articles of impeachment against Richard M. Nixon: obstruction of justice, abuse of presidential power, and noncompliance with the committee's subpoenas. Rather than face these charges on the House floor, Nixon resigned on August 9—the first president ever to have resigned from the country's highest office. In 1998, the House impeached William J. Clinton for obstruction of justice and perjury, but the Senate refused to convict on February 12, 1999. Both charges grew out of Clinton's effort to keep secret his sexual encounters with Monica Lewinsky, who at the beginning of their relationship was a young White House intern. A cartoon drawn by Jeff MacNelly for the *Chicago Tribune* alludes to the tawdry character of Clinton's conduct. It shows a naked Clinton, golf bag in hand, entering "The

Impeached Club." Nixon remarks to Johnson, "They let anyone in here these days." The cartoon not only places the Clinton impeachment controversy into historical context, but also hints that what Clinton did—lying about sex—was not worthy of impeachment.

On August 9, 1994, a special three-judge court appointed Kenneth Starr independent counsel to investigate Clinton's involvement in the Whitewater real estate deal. (An independent counsel is a prosecutor who investigates high executive wrongdoing independently of the Justice Department and the president.) Over the years, Starr's Whitewater investigation of Clinton grew into a multi-pronged effort to uncover the facts concerning the death of White House Deputy Counsel Vince Foster, the so-called Filegate and Travelgate, and the mysterious discovery of subpoened billing records in the private quarters of the Clinton White House. Clinton's defenders characterized Starr as a right-wing zealot out "to get the president."

A cartoon by Bill Garner that appeared on November 19, 1996, in the *Washington Times* indirectly disputes this characterization of Starr by comparing Clinton's paranoia to Nixon's. Though both presidents are clearly paranoid in the cartoon, the implication is that not all paranoid presidents are necessarily innocent. Nixon certainly was guilty of impeachable offenses and the bra hanging over Clinton's shoulder in the cartoon hardly places him in a good light.

Starr was eventually authorized to investigate whether perjury had been committed in the sexual harassment lawsuit that Paula Jones, a former Arkansas government employee, had filed on May 6, 1994, against former Governor Clinton. Jones claimed that Clinton crudely propositioned her in a hotel room in Little Rock on May 8, 1991. Clinton tried to get the case delayed on the constitutional ground that presidents while in office are absolutely immune from civil suit. Mark Thornhill for the *North County Times* of California drew an amusing cartoon

ARCHIBALD COX IS OUT TO GET ME!
KENNETH STARR IS OUT TO GET ME!
IT'S DEJA VU ALL OVER AGAIN!
© GARNER THE WASHINGTON TIMES '96

"TELL THE SUPREME COURT THAT PRESIDENTS DON'T HAVE TIME — HOT DAM, BIRDIE! — TO DEFEND THEMSELVES AGAINST LAWSUITS."

commenting on how Jones's lawsuit placed the National Organization for Women (NOW) in a quandary. Should NOW support a woman's right to sue a man who has arguably sexually harassed her or a president who, though accused of sexual harassment, has a strong record defending women's rights? It is hard to imagine a better way to mock the organization's ultimate decision, which was to support Clinton's request for a delay of the Jones case, than by Thornhill's juxtaposition of "NOW" and "LATER."

The case eventually came before the Supreme Court in *Clinton v. Jones*. Clinton's lawyers argued that a sitting president was too busy fulfilling his official responsibilities to defend himself in a private lawsuit. Jim Borgman for the *Cincinatti Enquirer* lampoons this argument in a cartoon of Clinton playing golf. The implication is that if Clinton has time to play golf, he has time to defend himself in a court of law. On May 27, 1997, the Court unanimously ruled against Clinton, rejecting the claim that he was too busy to defend himself in the Jones case and concluding that presidents could be sued for their private unofficial activities while they were in office.

In preparation for the upcoming trial, Jones's lawyers began the process of deposing witnesses. One of the people they wanted to depose was former intern Monica Lewinsky, who, it later came to be known, had had ten sexual encounters with Clinton from November 1995 to March 1997. On January 7, 1998, Lewinsky submitted to Jones's lawyers a legal affidavit denying that she had been sexually involved with Clinton. Jones's lawyers knew she was lying because Linda Tripp, Lewinsky's confidant and purported friend, had taped phone conversations in which Lewinsky told Tripp of her sexual encounters with the president. On January 17, the day after Starr was authorized to investigate whether perjury had taken place in the Jones case, Clinton denied under oath that he had ever had "sexual relations" with Monica Lewinsky or that he had ever been "alone" with her. In late July, Starr granted Lewinsky immunity in exchange for her testimony and cooperation. One piece of crucial evidence that Lewinsky turned over to Starr was a dress stained with semen that matched President Clinton's DNA. On August 17, 1998, in his testimony to a criminal grand jury, Clinton conceded that he had had an improper relationship with Lewinsky. In addition, he admitted that he had been misleading at his civil deposition, but he insisted that he had not committed perjury because oral sex did not fit the definition of "sexual relations" used in the Jones case.

After the House of Representatives voted to conduct an impeachment inquiry on October 8, the House Judiciary Committee held hearings during November and early December. Both politicians and ordinary citizens debated whether Clinton had committed impeachable offenses. Most Republicans argued that Clinton had committed perjury and obstructed justice, both felonies that clearly met the standard of a "high crime and misdemeanor." In response, many Democrats insisted that the case was really only about sex, a completely private matter not involving or affecting any of the president's public responsibilities or powers. If Clinton had told any lies, they were lies about consensual sex only, lies that had no relevance to whether Paula Jones had been sexually harassed in 1991.

On November 27, Clinton answered in writing eighty-two questions submitted to him by the House Judiciary Committee. A couple of weeks later, the committee recommended four articles of impeachment to the full House: perjury before the grand jury; perjury at the civil deposition; obstruction of justice; and, lastly, perjury in his answers to the committee's questions. On December 19, in sharply

partisan votes, the House impeached Clinton on the first article (228 in favor; 206 opposed) and the third (221 in favor; 212 opposed). Only five Democrats voted for one of the articles of impeachment, while only four Republicans voted against all the articles. Despite the partisan character of the votes, John Trever for the *Albuquerque Journal* drew a cartoon that placed the blame for the impeachment fiasco squarely on Clinton. It shows Congress, pictured as a Republican elephant, forcing a quivering Clinton to walk the "plank of impeachment." The plank, however, is not attached to a ship, but to a bridge Clinton himself has engineered: a "Bridge to the 21st Century." The reference is to a metaphor Clinton used in his acceptance speech for the presidential nomination at the Democratic National Convention in 1996. Promising to build a bridge to a better future for all Americans, Clinton in fact built one on

obstruction and perjury. It's a bridge leading not to the twenty-first Century, but, in Trever's view, to Clinton's political demise.

Despite the impeachment vote by the House, the American people, by a two-to-one margin, opposed Clinton's removal from office by the Senate. A majority even opposed his resignation from the presidency. On the other hand, most Americans felt that Clinton should be disciplined in some way for his conduct. One popular option was for the Senate to censure Clinton. Though the House Judiciary Committee had defeated such a motion on December 12, this option gained support among the general public. A majority of senators nonetheless felt that respect for constitutional precedent and the House of Representatives required a trial. On January 7, 1999, the Senate trial, with Chief Justice William H. Rehnquist presiding, began with a reading of the formal charges, but partisan procedural

disagreements quickly arose, especially on whether witnesses, including Monica Lewinsky, should testify before the full Senate. Not reaching consensus, the Senate set the issue aside and began, on January 14, to hear three days of argument by House prosecutors in favor of Clinton's removal, followed by three more days of argument by White House lawyers in favor of the opposite result. The American people's patience with the trial, as it rehashed what had already been in the public eye for months, quickly eroded, perhaps in part because it was becoming increasingly clear that two-thirds of the Senators were not going to vote to convict the president and remove him from office. An official censure of Clinton still seemed to be the most likely outcome. Jeff MacNelly for the *Chicago Tribune* drew a cartoon that aptly characterized the situation. The Senate is depicted as an old lady knitting a censure motion.

Clinton, standing nearby, asks impatiently, "Um . . . How long will this take?" and she responds, "Keep yer shirt on." What is especially amusing about the cartoon is that the yarn for the censure motion is coming from the legs of Clinton's pants. Once the motion is done, Clinton will occupy an embarrassing position in American history: a president without his clothes.

On January 26, the House prosecutors pared back their witness list to three individuals: Monica Lewinsky; Vernon E. Jordan, one of Clinton's closest friends; and Sidney Blumenthal, a White House aide. In the end, the Senate voted to depose these three witnesses on videotape. The dilemma of the Republican senators who wanted a quick end to the trial but felt they had to listen to some witness testimony is admirably captured in a cartoon by David Horsey drawn for the *Seattle Post-Intelligencer*. The Senate submits a question to Chief

Justice Rehnquist that calls to mind a familiar television advertisement of an elderly person who's fallen and can't get up. "Help!" the Senate cries, "I'm trapped in an impeachment trial and I can't get out."

After the videotaped depositions of Lewinsky, Jordan, and Blumenthal were taken, the House prosecutors indicated that they wanted to call only Monica Lewinsky to the stand, so that she could tell her story directly to the senators who were deciding Clinton's fate. Ignoring this request, the Senate on February 4 decided in bipartisan fashion (twenty-five Republicans joining the forty-five Democrats) not to hear any live testimony at the trial. Each side was permitted to use the videotaped depositions in a final review of the evidence, but that was all the testimony that would be taken by the Senate. Rob Rogers for the *Pittsburgh Gazette* drew a cartoon that dramatized the political fallout of the depositions and underlined the supreme irony of the Republican effort to impeach Clinton. With Chief Justice Rehnquist peering down from above, one Republican House prosecutor asks, "Were we able to inflict any damage by deposing witnesses?" Because the depositions uncovered no new significant information damaging to Clinton and because Clinton's approval ratings were never higher, one would expect the answer to be no. Instead, the other Republican, as he studies the polls, replies, "Yes . . . We destroyed our election hopes for 2000."

After one day of closing arguments and three days of closed deliberations, the Senate on February 12 finally voted to acquit President Clinton on both articles of impeachment. On the perjury charge, the vote was fifty-five to forty-five (all forty-five Democrats joined ten Republicans to vote against removal); on the charge of obstruction of justice, the vote was fifty to fifty (all forty-five Democrats joined five Republicans to vote against removal). Obviously, both votes fell well short of the sixty-seven votes (two-thirds of the Senate) needed to convict and remove a president from office. The country sighed in relief that the ordeal was finally over. ⚖

CHAPTER 21

Election 2000

Election 2000 was an extraordinary moment in American political and constitutional history. Though Americans cast their votes on November 7, the issue of who would succeed Bill Clinton as president remained unsettled for weeks afterward. It was clear that Democrat Al Gore had won the national popular vote by a slim margin, but Republican George W. Bush claimed that he had won a majority of the electoral votes. If Bush's claim was upheld, then he would win the election because the Constitution specifies that the president is to be selected by an Electoral College composed of electors chosen by state legislatures, each state choosing a number of electors equal to the number of senators and representatives it sends to Congress.

Currently, all state legislatures select electors based on the state's popular vote and all but Nebraska and Maine follow a winner-take-all rule: the candidate who wins the majority of the state's popular vote wins all the state's electoral votes. In election 2000, the crucial state was Florida and its twenty-five electoral votes. Bush had a slight lead in the Florida popular vote, but Gore demanded manual recounts of the ballots in four counties. Bush's team of lawyers fought back in both state and federal court. Eventually, to the surprise of many constitutional commentators, the issue of the constitutionality of the recounts found its way to the Supreme Court. Finally, on December 12, the Supreme Court ruled that the recounts had to stop, thereby insuring that Bush would keep Florida's elec-

toral votes. Never before in American history has a Supreme Court decision determined who would be president of the United States.

Over the course of American history, the institution of the electoral college has occasionally produced anomalous results. In 1800, Thomas Jefferson and Aaron Burr received an equal number of electoral votes, which threw the election into the House of Representatives and prompted the Twelfth Amendment that made ties impossible thereafter. In 1824, Andrew Jackson won the largest popular vote of four candidates, but failed to win a majority of the electoral votes, and lost the presidency after the House of Representatives selected John Quincy Adams. In 1876, Rutherford B. Hayes became president, even though Samuel J. Tilden won the popular vote, after a special commission recognized supporters of Hayes as the valid electors from South Carolina, Florida, and Louisiana, thereby giving Hayes a majority of the electoral votes. In 1888, Benjamin Harrison, despite losing the popular vote by a slim margin, defeated incumbent Democrat Grover Cleveland. In the twentieth century, the electoral college had functioned without incident until election 2000. Many Americans today nonetheless think that the electoral college is an antiquated part of the Constitution, one that is out of step with the country's evolving commitment to democracy. Chris Britt drew a cartoon for the *State Journal-Register* in Springfield, Illinois, that expresses this point of view. It calls the electoral college an antique that has no real value anymore.

Election night 2000 was a wild ride, both for the media and the candidates. Before 8 P.M. EST, and before all the polls had closed in Florida, the major television networks projected that Gore had beaten Bush in this battleground state. At about 2:15 A.M., the networks switched course, placing Florida in Bush's column and declaring him the winner. A

few minutes later, Gore called the Texas governor and conceded the election. Then, on his way to give his concession speech at a rally in Nashville, Gore learned from his advisors that Bush's lead in Florida had largely disappeared. Gore phoned Bush and retracted his earlier concession. At 4:15 A.M., the networks announced that Florida was simply too close to call and pulled their prediction that Bush had won the presidency. Mike Ramirez of the *Los Angeles Times* drew a scathing cartoon directed at the media's irresponsibility. In congressional hearings following the election, representatives of the media promised that they would never again predict a race while the polls were open.

Since Bush's margin of victory in Florida was initially only 1,784 votes, less than one-half of one percent of the nearly six million cast, Florida law required an automatic machine recount

of the ballots. While this recount was underway, Gore's lawyers searched for voting irregularities in Florida. They discovered that no votes were recorded on a significant number of Florida machine ballots: the so-called undervotes. Also, in Palm Beach County, a relatively liberal area, a large number of people had unexpectedly voted for Pat Buchanan, a conservative third-party candidate. Gore's team claimed that the voters had been confused by an unlawful "butterfly ballot" that placed the candidates in two columns on the right and left with a series of punch holes in a central column. Florida law required that paper ballots have a single column of candidates, with the place to mark one's vote positioned to the right of the candidate's name. Because of these discrepancies, there were calls for a new election in Palm Beach County. Mike Ritter drew a cartoon that seemingly mocked the attack on the legality of the butter-

fly ballot. It shows Gore racing over a sand dune chasing a "butterfly ballot" with his butterfly net at the ready. In response to Gore's allegations, Bush's lawyers quickly pointed out that the Palm Beach County ballot had been designed by a member of the Democratic Party, had been approved by officials of both parties, had appeared in local newspapers prior to the election, and did not have to coincide with the specific requirements of a paper ballot since it was a machine ballot.

On November 10, the machine recount was completed. Unofficially, Bush's lead had shrunk to 327 votes. At the request of Gore's lawyers, four Florida counties—Palm Beach, Dade, Broward, and Volusia—began a manual recount of the presidential votes. Secretary of State Katherine Harris, the state's chief elections official and a Republican who had co-chaired Bush's campaign in Florida, indicated that she would

not extend the statutory deadline for receiving election results. Except for absentee ballots coming from overseas, county election officials had to submit their results by 5 P.M. on November 14 or she would refuse to include them in her certification of the state's vote. After a state court judge confirmed that she had the discretion to decide whether to accept late returns, Harris indicated that she would not accept late returns unless there was proof of voter fraud, substantial noncompliance with election procedures, or an act of God (such as a hurricane) that prevented local officials from filing their returns on time. In her opinion, a confusing ballot, voter error, or the possibility that the outcome of the election might be effected were not weighty enough reasons to justify counting late submissions. Tom Toles drew a cartoon for the *Buffalo* (N.Y.) *News* that highlighted the paradox in Harris's reasoning: the country

SHOULD PREGNANT CHADS BE ALLOWED ABORTIONS!

DON'T START THAT!

ETC.

THEN IT WENT TO THE U.S. SUPREME COURT.

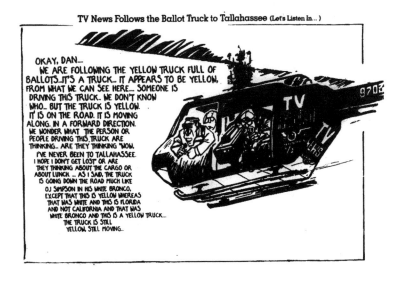

TV News Follows the Ballot Truck to Tallahassee (Let's Listen In...)

OKAY, DAN... WE ARE FOLLOWING THE YELLOW TRUCK FULL OF BALLOTS...IT'S A TRUCK... IT APPEARS TO BE YELLOW, FROM WHAT WE CAN SEE HERE... SOMEONE IS DRIVING THIS TRUCK... WE DON'T KNOW WHO... BUT THE TRUCK IS YELLOW. IT IS ON THE ROAD. IT IS MOVING ALONG... IN A FORWARD DIRECTION. WE WONDER WHAT THE PERSON OR PEOPLE DRIVING THIS TRUCK ARE THINKING... ARE THEY THINKING "WOW, I'VE NEVER BEEN TO TALLAHASSEE. I HOPE I DON'T GET LOST OR ARE THEY THINKING ABOUT THE CARGO OR ABOUT LUNCH... AS I SAID, THE TRUCK IS GOING DOWN THE ROAD MUCH LIKE OJ SIMPSON IN HIS WHITE BRONCO, EXCEPT THAT THIS IS YELLOW WHEREAS THAT WAS WHITE AND THIS IS FLORIDA AND NOT CALIFORNIA AND THAT WAS WHITE BRONCO AND THIS IS A YELLOW TRUCK... THE TRUCK IS STILL YELLOW. STILL MOVING...

might end up with "a president that the voters didn't elect." That in itself, Toles implied, was more than a sufficient justification for delaying the deadline so that the manual recounts could be completed prior to the certification of the election results.

On November 17, the Florida Supreme Court took the case and ordered Harris not to certify the election results. Four days later, the state's high court ruled that the manual hand counts could continue and gave the counties five days to complete them. During this time period, the American people learned a considerable amount about "chads"—the pieces of paper punched out of punchcard ballots. Chads not completely poked out could be left "hanging," "dimpled," or "pregnant." Counting machines would not tally some of these ballots, though a visual inspection of the ballot could arguably show for whom the voter intended to vote. Gore's hopes for victory depended on finding enough of these "undervotes" to overcome Bush's narrow lead, estimated unofficially at 286 votes on November 15. Cartoonists quickly took advantage of the laborious aspects of ballot inspection. Members of local canvassing boards were attempting to divine voter intent by various methods, including holding the ballots up to see if any light passed through any near-microscopic hole. After the United States Supreme Court agreed to hear Bush's appeal of the decision of the Florida Supreme Court, Universal Press-syndicated Pat Oliphant drew a cartoon picturing the justices analyzing each ballot in turn. The glazed looks on the justices' faces accurately captures the stultifying reality of a manual recount of hundreds of thousands of votes. It also hints at the underlying question of who was ultimately going to decide whether a ballot was or was not a legal vote: election officials, state judges, or justices on the Supreme Court?

HORSEY

· THE ONLY FIVE VOTES THAT COUNT ·

On November 26, after the state Supreme Court deadline expired, Harris certified Florida's election results, declaring Bush the winner by a margin of 537 votes. Since Palm Beach County did not complete its manual recount on time, Harris refused to include the county's results in the state totals. The next day Gore contested the certification in a circuit court in Tallahassee. On November 29, in the event that additional hand counts became necessary, N. Sanders Sauls, the judge selected to hear Gore's contest, ordered Palm Beach and Miami-Dade counties to deliver their million-plus ballots to the state's capitol. By this time, the media coverage of the events in Florida was approaching the saturation point. The *Los Angeles Times*'s Jeff Danziger

made this point artfully with a funny cartoon commenting on the media coverage of the yellow Ryder truck that conveyed the ballots to Tallahassee. The coverage had become so intense that it had become at times boring and more than slightly ridiculous.

On December 4, Judge Sauls upheld Harris's certification of Florida's election results. In the opinion accompanying the decision, Sauls explained that Gore had not met his burden of showing a "reasonable probability" that the manual recounts would affect the outcome of the state election. Gore immediately appealed Sauls's decision to the Florida Supreme Court. On the same day, the United States Supreme Court remanded Bush's original appeal back to the state's high court, asking the lower court for an explanation of why it had extended the time for manual recounts beyond the statutory deadline of November 14 when Article II of the federal Constitution says that state legislatures are to decide how a state chooses its presidential electors. In particular, the Supreme Court asked, what did the Florida court mean by saying that the legislature could not perform its function of determining the manner of selecting presidential electors in a way that would not impose "unreasonable or unnecessary" restraints on the right to vote protected by the Florida Constitution? The Supreme Court seemed to be hinting that the Florida Supreme Court could not extend the statutory deadline for manual recounts based on the state's constitution without running afoul of Article II.

On December 8, the Florida Supreme Court, in a divided 4 to 3 decision, overturned Sauls's decision and ruled that a statewide manual recount of presidential undervotes was the proper remedy for the contested election. In its opinion, the majority tried to avoid the Supreme Court's Article II objection by arguing that Florida's legislature had enacted an elections code that recognized the people's right to vote for presidential electors and granted courts the power to provide proper remedies in contested elections. The Florida court was therefore not circumscribing the authority granted to state legislatures by Article II, but rather acting pursuant to the very statutes that the state legislature had enacted based on its authority under Article II.

One day following the Florida Supreme Court's decision, the United States Supreme Court halted the manual statewide recounts in Florida by a vote of 5 to 4 and scheduled oral arguments for December 11. Operating with unprecedented speed, the Court issued its decision in *Bush v. Gore* on December 12. Again the Court split 5 to 4, with Chief Justice Rehnquist and Justices O'Connor, Kennedy, Scalia, and Thomas voting to end the recounts. The irony that five votes on a nine-justice court had settled the electoral controversy by insuring that an uncertain number of Florida voters would not have their votes counted became the subject of a cartoon drawn by David Horsey for the *Seattle Post-Intelligencer*. Over the caption "The Only Five Votes that Count," the five justices are smiling com-

placently, seemingly more than a little satisfied that the election was over and that Bush was president-elect.

In its opinion, the majority held that Florida's statewide recount of undervotes violated the Equal Protection Clause of the Fourteenth Amendment because local canvassing boards were left without any specific criteria of a legal vote other than the vague standard of "the intent of the voter." Moreover, the Supreme Court could not remand the issue of standards to the Florida Supreme Court for more clarification because Florida's legislature had expressed its desire to take advantage of the so-called safe harbor provision of a federal election law. According to this provision, a state could assure itself that its presidential electors would be permitted to vote in the electoral college if they were chosen by December 12. Since this date was the same day the Supreme Court handed down its decision, there was obviously no time for the Florida Supreme Court to fashion criteria of a legal vote that would meet constitutional standards and for a statewide recount to be completed. Time had run out.

Echoing the dissents filed in the case, commentators attacked the Court's decision in *Bush v. Gore* as a partisan move to deliver the election to Republican George W. Bush, an action completely at odds with the principle of an impartial judiciary. Criticism focused on the unprecedented character of the Court's extension of the Equal Protection Clause to the procedures of manual recounts in contested elections and certain language in the opinion that limited the decision "to the present circumstances." The fact that all the justices in the majority were conservative justices appointed by Republican presidents was also not overlooked. Jim Borgman drew a brilliant cartoon for the *Cincinnati Enquirer* that summed up these concerns. Reminiscent of a famous image of Marilyn Monroe from the film *The Seven-Year Itch,* it depicts the Supreme Court as a male judge standing on a subway grate with his robes billowing in the updraft. He has a shocked and bewildered expression on his face, presumably because everyone can now see that he has the feet of a Republican elephant!

Despite the criticisms of partisanship, the Court's decision in *Bush v. Gore* had the virtue of resolving a constitutional

BY BORGMAN FOR THE CINCINNATI ENQUIRER

WHEW!

impasse that might have turned into a constitutional crisis of major proportions. It is therefore arguable that the Supreme Court did the right thing. It may have sacrificed for a short time some of its legitimacy as the impartial umpire of the American system of government; however, by bringing the election to a close, it saved the country from a potentially harrowing experience. Jeff Koterba drew a cartoon for the *Omaha World Herald* that neatly captures this sentiment. Under a giant "WHEW," Uncle Sam collapses into his lounge chair now that "it's over." In such a close election, when the margin of victory was well within the margin of error, it's arguable that finality should have been the Court's primary consideration. 🖾

ACKNOWLEDGMENTS

This book began more than ten years ago as two separate projects on opposite ends of the country. As the two initiatives evolved and ultimately merged, we have been blessed by the enthusiastic support of countless friends and colleagues. On the West Coast, Maury Foreman, Harold Kahn, Hilary Casey, and Bruce Montgomery helped Mike gather and organize his personal collection of cartoons dealing with the Supreme Court and constitutional issues, perhaps the largest collection of its kind in the country. In Washington, D. C., while he was the Judicial Fellow at the Supreme Court from 1996 to 1998, Harry supervised an expansion of the Supreme Court's collection of political cartoons. The people who gave this opportunity to Harry and made the experience a rewarding one include the Commissioners of the Judicial Fellows Program, Chief Justice William H. Rehnquist, James C. Duff, Vanessa Yarnall, Charlotte Suniega, Gail Galloway, Catherine Fitts, Matthew Hofstedt, and the student interns who found and organized the hundreds of cartoons that were added to the Court's original collection: Sara P. Bryant, Andre Vanier, Jennifer Becker, Rachel DuFault, Ryan P. Green, Kimberly DeMarchi, Valerie Hays, Mary Hale, David Hollar, Martha Pacold, Eric Gottesman, Stephanie L. Kosta, Betsy Nahm, Ginger Anders, David J. Gunter II, and Genevieve Nadeau.

After our partnership was established, the project shifted from collecting cartoons to writing and editing this book. Along the way, we received unfailing courtesy and cooperation from numerous libraries, museums, newspapers, and archives. Sarah Schultz, Maureen Joyce, Victoria Kuhn, Athena Angelos, Mary Blake, Susan Kahn, Vincent DeMore, and Ian Walchesky tracked down countless details and kept the project moving forward. Both of us are extremely grateful to them for their conscientiousness, their good humor, and their valuable advice. Elaine and Bill Petrocelli have supported this project from the beginning, for which we are very grateful. A special thank-you goes to Patrick Allen, Thomas Payton, and Anne Boston, our editor, publisher, and designer at Hill Street Press respectively, for helping us get this book across the finish line.

We are also indebted to all the cartoonists who made this book possible, especially those who graciously gave us permission to use their work. This book is more the product of their creative energies than of ours. Our dedication of this book to them is in recognition of this reality. Finally, to our children, Matthew, Lauren, Katrina, and Nathan, and to our wives, Susan and Patricia, we can only say thanks for sharing our lives, including all the burdens and the joys of bringing this book to fruition.

ILLUSTRATION CREDITS

The editors and publisher are grateful to the following for permission to reproduce cartoons in their collections. Images may be protected by copyright. No images may be reproduced or distributed without their permission.

Chapter 9: Prohibition

p. 77, © 2002 *St. Louis Post-Dispatch*. Reprinted with permission of the *St. Louis Post-Dispatch*. All rights reserved.

p. 78, Fitzpatrick © 1926 *St. Louis Post-Dispatch*. Reprinted with permission of the *St. Louis Post-Dispatch*. All rights reserved.

p. 79, Rollin Kirby © 1925 *St. Louis Post-Dispatch*. Reprinted with permission of the *St. Louis Post-Dispatch*. All rights reserved.

p. 81, Fitzpatrick © 1933 *St. Louis Post-Dispatch*. Reprinted with permission of the *St. Louis Post-Dispatch*. All rights reserved.

Chapter 10: The New Deal

p. 85, © 1934 *St. Louis Post-Dispatch*. Reprinted with permission of the *St. Louis Post-Dispatch*. All rights reserved.

p. 87, Ino Cassals © 1935 *St. Louis Post-Dispatch*. Reprinted with permission of the *St. Louis Post-Dispatch*. All rights reserved.

p. 89, Fitzpatrick © 1935 *St. Louis Post-Dispatch*. Reprinted with permission of the *St. Louis Post-Dispatch*. All rights reserved.

p. 90, Fitzpatrick © 1935 *St. Louis Post-Dispatch*. Reprinted with permission of the *St. Louis Post-Dispatch*. All rights reserved.

p. 91, Elderman © 1935 *St. Louis Post-Dispatch*.Reprinted with permission of the *St. Louis Post-Dispatch*. All rights reserved.

Chapter 11: FDR's Court-Packing Plan

p. 97, Evans © 1937 *The Columbus Dispatch*. Reprinted with permission of *The Columbus Dispatch*. All rights reserved.

p. 99, Sykes © 1937 *Rochester Democrat & Chronicle*. Reprinted with permission of the *Rochester Democrat and Chronicle*. All rights reserved.

p. 100, Evans © 1937 *The Columbus Dispatch*. Reprinted with permission of *The Columbus Dispatch*. All rights reserved.

p. 101, Kendall Vintroux © 1937 *The Charleston Gazette.*Reprinted with permission of *The Charleston Gazette*. All rights reserved.

Chapter 12: Desegregation of Public Schools

p. 104, Fitzpatrick © 1954 *St. Louis Post-Dispatch*. Reprinted with permission of the *St. Louis Post-Dispatch*. All rights reserved.

p. 105, Bruce Shank © 1954 *The Buffalo Evening News*. Reprinted with permission of *The Buffalo Evening News*. All rights reserved.

p. 109, Fearing ©1969 *St. Paul Dispatch*. Reprinted with permission of the artist. All rights reserved.

Chapter 13: Prayer in Public Schools

p. 115, Burck © 1962 *Chicago Sun-Times* Reprinted with permission of the *Chicago Sun-Times*. All rights reserved.

p. 118, Tom Engelhardt © 1985 *St. Louis Post-Dispatch*. Reprinted with permission of the artist. All rights reserved.

p. 119, David Horsey © 1984 *Seattle Post-Intelligencer* Reprinted with permission of the *Seattle Post-Intelligencer*. All rights reserved.

Chapter 14: Watergate & Executive Privilege

p. 126, Jeff MacNelly © 1973 *The Richmond News Leader*. Reprinted with permission of Tribune Media Services. All rights reserved.

p. 127, Dick Locher © 1973 *Chicago Tribune*. Reprinted with permission of the *Chicago Tribune*. All rights reserved.

p. 129, Mike Peters © 1974 *Dayton Daily News*. Reprinted with permission of the *Dayton Daily News*. All rights reserved.

p. 131, Art Poiner © 1974 *Detroit News* Reprinted with permission of the *Detroit News*. All rights reserved.

Chapter 15: Abortion

p. 135, Tom Toles © 1989 *The Buffalo News*. Reprinted with permission of Universal Press Syndicate. All rights reserved.

p. 136, John Slade © 1989 *Louisiana Weekly* Reprinted with permission of the *Louisiana Weekly*. All rights reserved.

p. 139, Tony Auth © 1991 *The Philadelphia Enquirer*. Reprinted with permission of Universal Press Syndicate. All rights reserved.

p. 140, Jeff MacNelly © 1992 *Chicago Tribune*. Reprinted with permission of Tribune Media Services. All rights reserved.

Chapter 16: Equal Rights Amendment

p. 145 (left), McCarty © 1972 *San Bernardino Sun-Telegram*. Reprinted with permission of the *San Bernardino Sun-Telegram*. All rights reserved.

p. 145 (right), Eugene Craig © 1972 *Columbus Dispatch*. Reprinted with permission of the *Columbus Dispatch*. All rights reserved.

p. 146, Jack Bender © 1977 *Waterloo Courier* Reprinted with permission of the *Waterloo Courier*. All rights reserved.

p. 147, Etta Hulme © 1978 *Fort Worth Star-Telegram*. Reprinted with permission of the *Fort Worth Star-Telegram*. All rights reserved.

p. 149, Berke Breathed ©1988 *The Washington Post*. Reprinted with permission of the artist.

p. 151, Chuck Asay, © 1996 *The Colorado Springs Gazette*. Reprinted with permission of Creators Syndicate, Inc. All rights reserved.

Chapter 17: Affirmative Action

p. 154, Tom Engelhardt © 1977 *St. Louis Post-Dispatch*. Reprinted with permission of the *St. Louis Post-Dispatch*. All rights reserved.

p. 156, Tony Auth © 1989 *The Philadelphia Inquirer*. Reprinted with permission of Universal Press Syndicate. All rights reserved.

p. 157, Garner © 1995 *The Washington Times*. Reprinted with permission of *The Washington Times*. All rights reserved.

p. 159, Joseph Azar © 1996 *Legal Times Weekly*. Reprinted with permission of the *Legal Times Weekly*. All rights reserved.

Chapter 18: Free Press

p. 164, Don Hesse © 1972 *St. Louis Globe-Democrat*. Reprinted with permission of the *St. Louis Globe-Democrat*. All rights reserved.

p. 165, Patrick Oliphant © 1972 *Los Angeles Times*. Reprinted with permission of the artist. All rights reserved.

p. 167, Tom Engelhardt © 1978 *St. Louis Post-Dispatch*. Reprinted with permission of the author. All rights reserved.

p. 168, Etta Hulme © 1978 *Ft. Worth Star-Telegram*. Reprinted with permission of the *Fort Worth Star-Telegram*. All rights reserved.

Chapter 19: Flag Burning

p. 176, Hank McClure © 1990 *Lawton Constitution.* Reprinted with permission of the *Lawton Constitution.* All rights reserved.

p. 179, Pete Wagner © 1989 Reprinted with permission of the artist. All rights reserved. *www.wagtoons.com.*

p. 180, Jeff Stahler © 1990 *The Cincinnati Post.* Reprinted with permission of Newspaper Enterprise Association. All rights reserved.

p. 181, Chris Curtis © 1990 *Potomac Almanac.* Reprinted with permission of the *Potomac Almanac.* All rights reserved.

Chapter 20: The Clinton Impeachment Controversy

p. 184, Jeff MacNelly © 1999 *Chicago Tribune.* Reprinted with permission of Tribune Media Services. All rights reserved.

p. 185, Garner ©1996 *The Washington Times.* Reprinted with permission of *The Washington Times.* All rights reserved.

p. 186, Mark Thornhill © 1997 *North County Times.* Reprinted with permission of the *North County Times.*

p. 187, John Trever © 1998 *Albuquerque Journal.* Reprinted with permission of the *Albuquerque Journal.* All rights reserved.

p. 188, Jeff MacNelly ©1999 *Chicago Tribune.* Reprinted with permission of Tribune Media Services. All rights reserved.

p. 189, David Horsey © 1999 *Seattle Post-Intelligencer.* Reprinted with permission of the *Seattle Post-Intelligencer.* All rights reserved.

Chapter 21: 2000 Election

p. 194, Chris Britt © 2000 *State-Journal Register.* Reprinted with permission of the artist. All rights reserved.

p. 196, Mike Ritter © 2000 *The Sentinel.* Reprinted with permission of North America Syndicate. All rights reserved.

p. 197, Tom Toles © 2000 *The Buffalo News.* Reprinted with permission of Universal Press Syndicate. All rights reserved.

p. 198, Patrick Oliphant © 2000 *Patriot News.* Reprinted with permission of Universal Press Syndicate. All rights reserved.

p. 199, David Horsey © 2000 *Seattle Post-Intelligencer.* Reprinted with permission of the *Seattle Post-Intelligencer.* All rights reserved.

p. 202, Jeff Koterba © 2000 *Omaha World Herald.* Reprinted with permission of the *Omaha World-Herald.* All rights reserved.